Anything's Possible

Volume I

Anything's Possible

VOLUME I

MATT MILCHARD

StoryTerrace

Text Harry Cunningham, on behalf of StoryTerrace

Design StoryTerrace and Jelena Žarko

First print May 2021

StoryTerrace

www.StoryTerrace.com

CONTENTS

This book is dedicated to my loving family, especially my parents Carole and Michael whom I owe everything to. They are the most wonderful, loving and generous human beings I have ever met and I will be forever grateful for the unquestionable love, support and trust they have always given me throughout my life.

I truly love you with all my heart.

PROLOGUE: LATE FOR MY OWN DEATH

I have always found myself, inadvertently, at the centre of things. Life has never been short of excitement in that sense. Living many lives, I've had some close shaves and created plenty of drama myself over the years.

I shot an advert for the clothing brand Levi's in the 2000s. It involved me, a model in denim jeans and a jacket with a backpack containing a puppet called Flat Eric, on the run from a New York cop. It was however filmed in Kingston, London.

During the break, me and this New York cop walked into McDonald's to have a coffee on Kingston High Street. The next thing we know the McDonalds is slowly emptying around us. Within a few minutes, the whole place was empty. We were the only ones upstairs.

"Do you reckon we've upset everyone?" the guy playing the cop said to me.

"Maybe our costumes have scared everybody off."

Then, suddenly without warning, real police dressed in all the riot gear and carrying guns, bound up the stairs to the McDonalds and ordered us on the floor. An armed response team followed up and we were treated like terrorists, pinned against the floor and then led away. This was surely a horrifying mistake. Had we been set up? At that moment, my body pressed hard against the floor I felt sure I was going to get shot for real. We were taken away downstairs and carted into the back of a police van, without a bullet being fired. I was terrified.

What had really happened was my friend playing the cop had taken out his fake gun and placed it on the table while he drank his coffee. Being an American where everyone can have a gun in public, he'd not thought twice about it. It was an innocent mistake but one which led to a huge drama. Somebody in McDonald's had obviously spotted the prop gun and phoned the police telling them there was a gunman on the prowl. They let us go after a few minutes of high drama in the police van.

Conversely, I have often found myself on the fringes of danger. On the morning of the 7/7 bombings in London when I was in my early thirties, I decided I would go to the gym instead of heading into my office at the usual time. Little did I know that changing my mind saved my life. I would have picked up the tube heading to Aldgate East and would have been on the train where the first bomb exploded. Aldgate East is a two-minute walk to Brick Lane where my offices were.

When I eventually came to get on the tube an hour or so later to head to work, I got halfway through my journey and was forced to evacuate because of the threat. Being in London on that day was initially horrible. Police cars were zooming everywhere, people were panicking, and the sense of terror and tension sat thick in the air. There was also an excitement to it, that rush of adrenaline as you just reacted to events. There is a morbid uncertainty to that moment. You have no idea if there's going to be another attack. The attack that I experienced could have been just the start of something much bigger. The next few months were awful. I stopped taking the tube. I drove in, which in London is ridiculous, it's much slower and the parking is expensive.

The second time I narrowly avoided death in London was in 2013. I was working as a mixed-martial-arts teacher at Mulgrave Primary School at the time and the playground is next to Woolwich Barracks. I was heading there one day with my business partner and co-founder of Pyramid Martial Arts, Jamie, and we were late. The school were very funny about teachers being late for after-school clubs, so we usually made a point of being there early. On that particular day, we were behind schedule. All the roads were gridlocked, and we couldn't understand it. Our kickboxing gym was only five minutes away, but we were panicking, knowing full well that the headmaster would be annoyed that we were late for the lesson. We phoned up the school and no one answered. Once again helicopters were flying around us and we got nervous phone calls from our friends asking us where we were and if we were okay.

The soldier, Lee Rigby, had been attacked and murdered outside the school by two extremists and the kids, waiting for their afterschool clubs in the playground, had seen all of it. It is horrific to think about. Once again, I had pause to think about how close I came to being in the middle of it all. We were dressed in instructor's uniforms, donning black belts. Had we been there I am sure that we would have been expected to jump in and disarm the extremists. I don't know how well we would have fared. I often look back on all these incidents and wonder whether someone was looking out for me.

You could say throughout my life I have been late to my own death and I hope to operate in that tardy manner for a long time yet!

1

SURVIVING A COUP

I am a very calm person. My parents, Michael and Carole are similar. That might be because I've been involved in so many hair-raising, sticky situations that now I am able to just take it all in my stride.

I grew up living in Jakarta during the 1980s. As a young child, my parents shielded me and my sister Charlotte from much of the dark side of Indonesia. Today it's a comparatively open place. When you think about Indonesia your first thought is Bali which is seen as a tourist's paradise. Back then however even Bali, which we often visited at the weekends like it was Butlins, had very few foreigners. Whilst the country was politically unstable, the kind of life you could live there as a foreigner was one of luxury and a world away from where I was born in Romford, Essex.

We had drivers to take us everywhere and guards outside our home so the dark side wasn't something we encountered daily. But there were a few incidents that seemed to occur out-of-the-blue that you had to deal with.

The most memorable of those incidents was the day terrorists launched a coup on the Indonesian capital of Jakarta. On the night it occurred you could hear guns going off all over the city and the skies were ablaze with missiles, flying over the compound where us ex-pats lived. The militants were aiming for a nearby munitions dump.

We were extremely lucky as a family and lived in a palatial house that had floor to ceiling windows. Beautiful in normal circumstances. Not so helpful in the middle of a coup! It was like living in a greenhouse. The missiles flew past us and the house shook with the force of every explosion, getting nearer and nearer. A few close calls led to the glass blowing out of their pains. The fear of not knowing whether me or my family would survive if a bomb landed closer, or if the attackers would enter the house hung over us throughout the siege. As a 10-year-old, this was a horrific situation to be in. My mum, dad, sister Charlotte, and I hid in our bedroom on the opposite side of the house, barricaded in. We picked up the mattresses and hoisted them up against the windows to cushion us against the thousands of tiny pieces of glass that would have otherwise gone flying towards us as the windows shattered. We could still hear everything from under the bed. It was terrifying.

We had no idea whether we'd be able to stay in the city, whether we'd have to go into hiding or the embassy would evacuate us. Nothing seemed to phase my mum and dad however, so I know I wasn't as scared as I could have been. They're just not the sort of people who panic.

Another one of these incidents was when the same extremist group decided they were going to kill all the foreigners in Jakarta they saw on the streets whilst I was at school. The official threat was delivered via the Indonesian press.

Bloody Imperialists

We charge you with the murder of thousands of Muslims at the hands of your butcher...

Any US, French, Italian or British establishment or citizens may become our targets at any time and place.

The teachers rounded us up and took us in a convoy across the city to the embassy where we had to hide. As a kid when you're with your friends, most of whom were also from an international background, it did feel more like an adventure than it should have. I think it helped us mask how scary the reality was.

Thankfully, none of these incidents came to pass and things calmed down for the rest of my time there. Looking back though, our family was stalked by bad luck right from the start of our time in Indonesia. My father was a consultant who helped developing countries create essential oils with lime and pepper. We first arrived there when I was around 10, we were put up in a hotel while my parents decided where we would live more permanently. Once, after a hard day spent house-hunting, looking at the phenomenal properties that you could afford as a Westerner, there was a man who robbed us blind of our valuables. He had climbed in to our room via the air vent tunnels that ran between all the rooms and waited inside, observing our every move, watching where we stashed our money and other precious items. When we got back from house-hunting, we went down to dinner at the hotel and by the time we came back everything had gone.

My first ever computer, my sister's treasured eraser collection and her jewellery, all stolen. It was unsettling not just for the loss of material possessions but because someone had been in my room spying on me. As soon as I found out we'd been robbed, I ran down the corridor of the hotel, with a little pen knife, trying to get the guys who did it. Most of our big possessions were still being shipped over from the UK. So, we were lucky in that sense. For a few days however, we had nothing.

Whilst we settled into our new house we also had to get used to having a full-time cleaner, chef, guard and chauffeur that lived with us in separate quarters at the rear of the house. You were sharing your space with these people, which was hard when you were a kid. They were just strangers to me at first and it took time for them to become like family to us, which before long, they did.

Healthcare was often problematic as well. Ordinarily, the British embassy would fly my Dad or any of us out to Singapore if we needed serious medical treatment because the hospitals in Indonesia were not of the same quality. When my appendix burst we didn't have time to get on a flight. I had to have the operation in a public hospital in Jakarta. There were so many stories amongst the ex-pat community about how bad the healthcare system was in Indonesia.

"Don't ever have an operation in Jakarta," one of the other families said, "because they'll probably leave half the equipment inside you!"

I went to Jakarta International School, but it was very American. I developed an American accent and quickly lost any interest in playing football after I saw everyone else reaching for baseball bats during lunchtime. We learned Indonesian in school and I became fluent very quickly. I could still have a decent conversation with you in it today with a bit of practice. It didn't help us settle into the wider society. The barriers we faced with the outside world wasn't to do with the language, they were cultural.

I don't think this was confined to Indonesia. The whole region was politically unstable back then. We used to travel around at weekends on holidays. We were flying to Singapore once but mid-flight we were diverted to Bangkok. They took us all straight off the plane when we landed, and we had to slide down those emergency chutes. We were all rushed to the terminal as fast as we could. You could see people panicking, and you had no idea what was going on. There was a bomb on board the plane. Somebody called it in and thankfully it didn't go off. It was just one more example of how close you came to death living in Asia at that time.

How sweet and innocent? Seychelles

JAKARTA INTERNATIONAL SCHOOL
MEMORANDUM

To : ALL STAFF AND ALL PARENTS

Date : March 27, 1984

From : Clarence L. Dilts, Superintendent

Subject : THREATS TO PERSONAL SAFETY

Within the past few days the following letter has appeared in the Indonesian press and the four named Embassies have received copies.

"In the name of Allah, the Compassionate, the Merciful

Bloody Imperialists:

We charge you with the murder of thousands of Muslims at the hands of your butcher - our Zionist enemy in Lebanon and Palestine, on the Golan Heights and Sinai. You have supplied Tel Aviv with funds, modern weapons and guaranteed international political support for its actions. Nowadays your troops in Lebanon are murdering women, old people and children only because they are faithful Muslims.

We cannot treat your bloody crimes with indifference. Therefore we shall wage a merciless war against you with your methods. From now on neither you nor your wives and children will find peace on Muslim soil. Any U.S., French, Italian or British establishments /or citizens may become our targets at any time and place.

Developments in Beirut and Kuwait indicated that fleets of warships and aircraft cannot ensure your security. We are capable of punishing you everywhere.

Our sacred duty is to take revenge on you for the suffering and blood of Muslims! And we shall be revenged! Murder for murder! Allah is with us!

Islamic Jihad."

ALL ITEMS OF THIS SORT MUST BE TREATED SERIOUSLY. AT JIS WE HAVE TAKEN APPROPRIATE ACTION AS REGARDS CAMPUS SECURITY AND OUR TRANSPORTATION SYSTEM.

Letter in Jakarta from Extremists

Helping myself to a chicken?

Our back garden in Seychelles with my notorious bike

'Borrowing' the neighbours Puppy for a few days

Dad with our dogs Pepsi and Patch in Jakarta

Missiles flying over our house during the uprisings in Jakarta.

Playing baseball for the little league in Jakarta

Mum, Dad and Me in Seychelles

Voyaging the seas on a small fishing boat to camp on a volcano 'Anak' Krakatoa

Camping trip on uninhabited active volcano 'Anak' Krakatoa.

2

EVERYWAY BUT ESSEX

My father's contract in Jakarta ended when I was 12 or 13, and we were soon on our way back to England. We left behind some pets and all of my friends; I was finishing one life and moving on to another.

The transition was also hard because I was moving away from a palatial environment and back into a comparatively modest house in Billericay, Essex. This was also a problem because I enrolled in a private grammar school called St John's. The kids there saw me being picked up by my parents in a modest car while they all came to school in Bentleys and I soon realised that I wasn't of the same status as they were. I also had an American accent, and everyone leapt at the chance to mock me for it. To the kids at St John's, it didn't make any sense. It was immensely difficult as I was made to feel like an outsider and that my experiences of life in Jakarta were made up to impress them. I knew a handful of people, friends from when I lived in England before, but it was clear I didn't fit in here.

Those first few weeks were such a huge shock. St John's only had a few-hundred students, so it was very insular. The curriculum at St John's was also very typical of an English private school, a rigid course with very little freedom. If a teacher walked in the room, you had to stand up and there was also a strict uniform.

The most sinister element of this school was the headmaster, a strange but traditional man who wore a mortar cap and gown. You'd quiver uncontrollably if he walked into a room, frightened he might call you out on something or take you away. He taught one lesson a week, Spanish. Throughout the lesson he'd have his hands placed firmly in his pockets jingling his keys. If you had a low-test score or you broke the rules, there were rumours that you'd get called into his private study for what the kids called a 'bum rub'. One day, I got a low score on one of his Spanish tests and I was called to his office. As I walked in, I noticed the moose heads on the wall and oak panelling; it looked like a set from an old-fashioned movie. Nobody likes going to the headmaster's office anyway, but I had no idea what to expect or what was waiting for me on the other side of his office door.

"Put your head on the desk," he said. My stomach sank. I was fully expecting to get a beating. I braced myself. Instead, I got this gentle, weird, rubbing of my bum which went on for a few seconds before he told me to leave and not to get a low score ever again.

I didn't think much of it that night other than it was a weird experience, amusing in some ways. But the day following that incident a police car turned up at school and the headmaster was taken away in handcuffs in view of all the students. All the power he'd once held over us disappeared. It transpired afterwards that I was one of the lucky ones. He'd done far worse with some of the other boys. There was a trial in which some of my classmates had to testify and as far as I'm aware he was sent to prison.

It made school a weird, unsafe environment. On the day the headmaster was taken away all the teachers played it down. If any of the students were caught talking about it, the conversation would be immediately ended.

I continued to struggle with the teasing at St John's, feeling increasingly isolated as time went on. That was at least until one of the kids who had continued to torment me about my accent and my lack of status, Leon, told everyone he was going to wait for me at the end of the day.

The whole school were talking about it and were looking forward to seeing me get my head kicked in. They gathered around the playground in a pack as he geared up to fight me. I felt sick with fear. I didn't understand why he felt the need to hurt me. Leon rounded on me and boxed me into a corner of the playground until there was nowhere left to go. Everyone was chanting and jeering, egging him on to hit me.

He hit me in the head.

"I'm not fighting," I'd say back and then he'd hit me again. The crowd were going crazy. But my blood was boiling.

"I don't want to fight you," I said again, but I no longer believed the words that were coming out of my mouth and all of a sudden, I saw my instincts took over, turned around and knocked him out first with a crashing jab to his nose followed by a devastating uppercut to his jaw. He dropped with an outburst of gasps and cheers from the onlooking crowd. That was the first time I'd hit anyone.

Time stood still. I wondered if I had hurt him badly and the questions started to fly through my mind. Would he get back up? Would I be expelled? Were things going to change?

Within an instant, everything switched. He started crying, his nose bled, and everyone was instead looking at me in a new way. Everyone was shocked that I'd hit back but there was a newfound respect that they had for me. There was also a change that happened inside me. I felt more confident like I'd taken off my invisibility cloak. The bullies started to leave me alone and the girls who'd once teased me now actually seemed interested in me.

I think Leon was just trying to jockey for position and ensure he was taken seriously by other people in the school. After that incident, we became good friends. Years later he reached out to me and bizarrely invested in one of my businesses.

At the end of the school year, as I prepared to take my GCSEs, things changed a lot. I was more confident, my friendship circles had changed, and my time at St John's and in Essex was coming to an end. I moved to Canterbury as my Dad's company was relocating and managed to blag my way into one of the top sixth forms in the area; Simon Langton Grammar School for Boys.

It was a miracle I got into Simon Langton because when my GCSE results came out, they were not pretty. I got 3 grades above C. My parents were disappointed. They'd spent all this money on my education and I'd left with very little to show for it. The school, however, saw potential in me and agreed to let me in for A-Levels in Maths, Economics and Sociology if I retook my GCSEs simultaneously. I wanted to make it up to my parents and so I knuckled down to get both my GCSEs and A-levels.

When I first started at the sixth form, it was an unnatural situation to find myself in. I was the newcomer in a school that most of the other students had attended for their whole lives. They all knew each other, and I was a stranger. This time however, I wasn't going to make the same mistakes again. With my newfound confidence, I initially made friends with a group of not so popular kids, I guess that you might call them nerds! It was easier to fall in with them but it was like déjà vu as the tougher kids started to pick on me. I was kicking a football around with these friends who'd welcomed me with open arms, and standing on the other side of the playground was a group of kids just chucking apples at us. Sixth formers in those days were more like kids than they are today. There were three of them.

Jon and Garrick stood well over 6 feet tall who proudly showed their enthusiasm for weightlifting through their physicality. Andy on the other hand was 5 foot and thin to match. That didn't mean he wasn't a force to be reckoned with however. He was extremely mischievous.

Jon was the ringleader of that group and when he chucked an apple at me, I was not going to have it. I grabbed the apple and threw it straight back at him. It was like walking into a club and suddenly the DJ cut the music and the lights had gone up. Everybody froze and wondered what was happening. I was nervous. I feared that I had personally signed my death certificate by engaging with these kids.

Once again, my reaction seemed to garner a certain level of respect. All of a sudden, I was in with the cool kids which transformed my transition straight away; now I was part of the clique. What was nice was that after this incident I managed to bring some of the first crowd, the nerds, over to the cool group. There was this blend that took place because of me. I never ignored the nerds. I would invite them to all the parties and beckon them over to sit with me at the cool table at lunch. I ended up having a nice big group of friends. I think this had a positive effect on other people as well.

When I first started, I made friends with an Indian guy, Umesh, who was so shy he couldn't even talk to people. Towards the end, I invited him to all the parties, and he came out of his shell; he became quite a comical figure.

Jon, Andy and Garrick became three of my best friends. I'm still very close with Jon and Garrick today but Andy sadly passed away while we were at school. He had cystic fibrosis. Because he knew he was going to die he didn't care at all about what he said or what he did; he was a rebel to everyone and everything. He was an inspiration who knew how to live. If he were bored in a class, he would just walk out. He was also the biggest 'shit-stirrer' you could find; he was probably the one that told Jon to throw the apple at me in the first place.

One night I was with Andy and a big group of friends and we were at a house party, staying overnight because the girl's parents had gone away. Canterbury is very much an army town. We headed out for a walk at 2am and it was snowing. On the other side of the road, there's someone from the army in uniform walking with their girlfriend.

They'd been out drinking and had a row. Andy being Andy decided taunt him but the squaddie overheard the conversation. He hit his girlfriend in front of us and then declared, "You two are next!"

I gulped. What had Andy started? Andy was in hysterics and the squaddie came over, provoked. But Andy legged it, leaving me to fend for myself. The squaddie pushed me to the ground and once again I found myself fighting. We were rolling around someone's front garden in the early hours of the morning. I gave as good as I got and when we got up, we were both covered in blood.

Where is Andy? I thought, the coward! The army guy then threw me up against the car, and suddenly I had his knife in my mouth. I couldn't move or speak.

"Give me your car," the squaddie demanded. I try to tell him that I was only 16 I didn't even have a car.

In the moonlight, I can just see Jon running down the road coming to my rescue. Andy had told him what had happened and there he was, brandishing a huge carving knife in hand that he had grabbed from the kitchen drawer at the party, chasing away this squaddie. Whether the squaddie really intended to do me any real harm or he'd just got this knife in my mouth to stop the fight as I was getting the better of him, I will never know. This was typical of what would happen if you hung around with Andy and his big mouth. He'd always run away and me, Garrick and Jon would be the ones left in the line of fire.

On another notable occasion, Andy, Garrick, and I were driving around in my first car; a flash MG Turbo. I bought it soon after I turned 17 and passed my test. As we were driving along, Andy decided to open his window and shout something out to a group of men walking back from the pub. I closed his window and told him to pipe down, thinking no more of it. Much later we had to pull into an Esso garage to get some petrol. As I was filling up the car to my horror, this same group of lads turned the corner and started walking towards the garage obviously peckish after a good night drinking. I lowered my cap and carried on filling up hoping they would not recognise the car. A foolish hope!

The ringleader started walking over and before I knew it, he had opened the passenger door and begun laying into Andy. Garrick who would usually have handled a situation like this with ease had slipped a disc in his lower back and couldn't get out of the car to come to Andy's rescue. Before I knew it, I had flown around the side of the car back into the line of fire though I was just as concerned that my new car wouldn't get damaged in the battle as I was about Andy. I pulled the assailant off Andy and threw him into his friends to stop them from jumping me as well. The guy held up his hands, told me to calm down and said the fight was over. He then whispered something to me. I couldn't hear what he said so I leaned in closer but as I did, he drew back and headbutted me squarely in the face, breaking my nose. It was a lesson of trust I would remember for the rest of my life.

By the time I had realised what had happened the group were legging it and the attendant from the petrol station announced over the tannoy that the police were on their way. Yet another trip in an ambulance and my poor parents experienced yet another call in the middle of the night to tell them I had got myself in another tangle.

In the final year of school, Andy sadly passed away. He always knew he was going to die, as did we, but he never got to finish his A-Levels. When you're 17 or 18 you don't expect to see one of your daily friends pass away.

Sadly, Andy wasn't the only person I was close with who died when I was in sixth form. I started dating the next-door neighbour's daughter, Leigh. She was a bit of a tomboy at heart, though she didn't look like one, and we'd gotten together after being friends for a while. She'd kick footballs around, and she looked a bit like Julia Roberts. It was around the same time that Pretty Woman came out. It cemented my reputation as the cool kid, having just seen off the hard kids throwing apples at me I now had this beautiful girlfriend. Leigh's sister was dating another guy called Nick and the four of us would often go out together. One night he never turned up when we'd arranged to hang out. He wasn't answering the phone and Leigh's sister thought she'd been stood up. She was angry for a while, Leigh and I were trying to calm her down, thinking he'd just lost his phone or he was late. In fact, he'd had a brain aneurysm and dropped dead as he was running for the train to come and meet us.

I lost two good friends my age that year and it brought it home to me that life is fragile, and you just never know what is around the corner.

I got the A-levels I was required to get in maths, economics and sociology and I met the challenge of completing my 5 GCSEs as well. I found numbers quite straight forward to deal with so maths was a good choice. God knows why I chose sociology, but I took economics because the headmaster advised me to, it was his subject, and he was keen for me to do it as a requirement of me getting into the school. I was glad that he did because the subjects were enough to get me a place at the University of Greenwich reading Building Surveying. It would all stand me in good stead as I began to think about the future and where my business interests might take me.

Headmaster is accused

HEADMASTER of Billericay's St John's School, Mr Alan Greenstein, was accused of indecent assault on a boy, when he appeared at Billericay Magistrates' Court on Friday.

Mr Greenstein, 48, of Westcliff-on-Sea, was remanded on bail. Bail conditions are that he remains at his home address and does not attempt to visit St John's School.

The alleged offence was said to have taken place in December 1985. Mr Greenstein is due to appear at court again on March 27.

● St John's private school was opened in Stock Road, Billericay, 60 years ago.

There are about 370 pupils, girls and boys, aged between four and 18.

Fees range from £440 to £600 a year, for a "basic traditional education," the curriculum has changed very little over the years, though 1983 saw the introduction of two new subjects, computer studies and Spanish.

St John's is a member of the Independent School Association Incorporated, which notes the school for its high academic standard and strict standards of appearance.

The school was built in seven-and-a-half acres of land and pupils are encouraged to make the most of the sports facilities, stressing the importance of traditional team games such as hockey, rugby and football.

This year's examination results at the school were described as the "best ever" with 'O'-level candidates gaining an average of six passes each at grades A, B and C.

Headmaster, Mr Greenstein, said recently he was very proud of pupils' academic achievements.

Police are called to MP's flat

POLICE were called to Billericay and Wickford MP Harvey Proctor's London flat on Tuesday after an incident involving the MP and another

man said on Thursday: "The complainant has not made a formal complaint apart from calling the police at the time of the disturbance."

My Headmaster arrested and imprisoned for Child abuse - I had a narrow escape.

St Johns, Billericay

3

BACHELOR OF SCIENCE, MASTER OF PROPERTY, JACK OF ALL TRADES

The faith that my parents and Simon Langton had shown in me had paid off and after a summer of freedom I started the next stage of my life studying Building Surveying at the University of Greenwich. I'm very much a person who likes to prove people wrong. So, when a teacher at St John's said to me "you're not an academic but you'll go far in business" it made me even more determined to get a degree. Greenwich was only an hour from my parents in Canterbury, so I didn't feel as if I had moved so far. Most of my friends also went to university. Garrick went off to Plymouth and Jon went to a university in London.

When I look back, studying only took up a very small part of my time at Greenwich. I was involved with a number of other projects alongside my academic work.

To start with there was my modelling. After my younger sister, Charlotte, started modelling and acting she managed to get me signed up to her agent. I appeared in magazines like Chat or Take a Break as the model for some of the real-life stories they ran. After a while I got a fairly regular gig modelling for the 'Dear Deidre' column in The Sun. There'd be a photo casebook, a kind of comic strip where a person's problems would be laid out and Dearie would offer her advice. I'd usually be photographed in bed with my top off or having an arguing with someone. Although magazines like Chat had a large readership, no one at university was bothered with them. If I were in The Sun however, even though I didn't tell anyone, everyone would know about it. I'd walk onto campus that day and somebody would have taken it upon themselves to cut out the column and pin to the noticeboard of the lecture hall. It was all harmless banter, of course, but I'd always be ducking out of lectures to go and do as many modelling jobs as I could.

Then there were my business aspirations. I'd been running businesses since the age of 10. I sold homemade garden gnomes at car boot sales or designed business cards and letterheads for local businesses when I was still at Simon Langton. By the time I got to university, I already knew how to get a business off the ground.

I spotted an opportunity at university straight away. There wasn't a martial arts club there that I thought was any good. Having trained in martial arts since I was a kid, I decided to solve that problem by setting up my own. I approached the Students' Union for a grant, and they gave it to me. I rented the sports hall and ran the club there for my entire time at university. We had about 50 students in total, which was a great way for me to make new friends.

I was big into solving problems. Another problem I wanted to rectify was not wanting to waste money by renting a student flat or house in London. So, I found a big house in Greenwich and got together with Garrick and another one of my friends, Joey.

We had no idea how on earth we were going to get a mortgage for a couple of hundred grand. Through our combined talents, we somehow managed to get the deposit together. It was a perfect combination. Garrick had some savings, I was earning good money from the modelling and Joey had an amazing way with words. Between the three of us, we pulled it off.

Since this house was huge, we converted the garage and some of the rooms and turned it into a seven-bedroom house which we were able to do largely ourselves because we were all doing construction degrees. This was enough space for us to live in and some extra rooms to rent out to help pay the mortgage. That was the start of my property empire. It was in an up-and-coming area and we knew that our investment would pay off eventually.

As the first housing project was going so well, I invested in another one on the same street. I realised there was a niche here. Joey and Garrick stayed out of the second one, but my father gave me some help and we just kept going.

By the time I'd finished university, I had 6, three-storey 5-bedroom houses all on the same street and two luxury apartments in Docklands.

Students were just the first group of people to occupy my houses. As I did more and more modelling work and went further down that path, I started to realise there was a niche for people looking to make it in the acting and modelling world who needed a base in London. In offering them a house I was able to create a network of other budding creatives. For them, the appeal was like living in students' halls rather than living on their own in flats dotted around London. The only advertising I needed to do was in The Stage, a magazine just for aspiring performers.

Of course, the fact that I owned several houses whilst at university helped with my reputation, as too did being the martial arts instructor who owned the club. Most of my socialising was based around this. Although I might appear to have been flash and extravagant, I worked hard for the life I wanted. I also had a part-time job as a lifeguard at the local sports centre. I didn't want to be the typical student who goes out drinking all the time, slacking off.

My modelling for the newspapers and "real-life" magazines at university was a gateway into other projects. Modelling led to dancing at a club called Zen's in Dartford and Amadeus in Rochester with my good friend Tony. I enjoyed it so much I wanted to learn how to dance properly. I started taking lessons with a man called Len Goodman. While today he is very famous for Strictly Come Dancing when I took lessons with him in the late '90s he wasn't known at all.

It was an interesting experience, and it was quite unusual. I was 20 and this is generally regarded as quite old to start dancing. I was also the only boy in the class. All the girls turned around to look at me and it was clear they wondered what on earth I was doing there. I didn't socialise or mix with any of them. Maybe I was embarrassed about how bad I was to start with. The truth was that when I started, I was rubbish. With Len's help however, I found the confidence to continue and improve. He was a really lovely man, exactly as he is on the telly today.

The first couple of lessons were quite daunting. I couldn't pick up the routines but after a while, I got into it and started to enjoy it. It helped my career and my dancing at Zen's and various other London clubs took off to the point that by the time I left university I had an offer for a job dancing in Vienna.

Looking back on my life at university I had a great and fun time. I proudly managed to prove my teachers wrong and get a 2:1 in Building Surveying. By the time it all came to an end I was already itching to dive straight into a new challenge; Vienna was calling me.

Proud Graduation - BSC Hons Degree in Building Surveying.

4

VIENNA

I auditioned for a job as a backing dancer at a posh club in Vienna. Auditions were held at the world-famous Pineapple Dance Studios in London and the routines I had to learn were intricately choreographed. I was used to a freestyle approach during auditions, so this was a new experience for me. I was up against many seasoned professionals and didn't expect that I would get far.

When I was told I'd got the job I was elated. There was just one problem. I hadn't yet finished my degree. I had to ask my university for an extension. Just two days after I finished my degree I jumped on a plane, went straight to Vienna and left my life in London far behind.

On my arrival however, things were not right. The company who had hired me were supposed to meet me at the airport and take me to my accommodation. I was picked up by a black limo and the driver, who looked more like a bodyguard, could hardly speak any English. I wanted to know where we were going but we were unable to have any kind of intelligible conversation. He dropped me, not at a plush hotel, but at a hostel in the middle of nowhere. My room was made up of a single bed and little else. There was no toilet and I could hear shouting in the room next to me. I began to wonder if I had made a huge mistake. It was a Saturday and the driver indicated, somehow through the impenetrable language barrier, that he would pick me up on Monday and that I would have a day to spare in Vienna.

When I woke up the next morning it was like something out of the film Hostel. There were drug dealers and people I didn't feel comfortable around in other rooms. I felt vulnerable, I didn't know whether it was safe to leave my belongings in the room. It left me feeling immediately homesick. I had taken a huge step outside of my comfort zone to follow this exciting opportunity, but I wondered whether it had all been a huge mistake.

In the end, I made a beeline for the city itself, aiming to spend as little time as possible in the hostel. When I tried to get breakfast, however, everything was closed including the supermarkets because it was a Sunday. No one could speak English. I felt underprepared, isolated and lost. I did the only thing I could think of in the moment. I phoned my mum.

"I hate it," I said, "I want to come home." My mum was sympathetic but rational and practical as always.

'What do you want us to do?' she asked.

They were very good at calming me down. All I had to

do, they explained, was try to get some food, go back to bed and wait to see what tomorrow would bring. I found a local market and bought some cheese and bread and then went and hid in my room, locking myself in. The agent in England wouldn't answer. No one came to pick me up on Monday morning. I didn't have a mobile phone with me, so I was using a payphone. I was worried that this wasn't a legitimate job and that I'd flown out to a foreign country for no reason. Eventually, on Monday, I got hold of the agent and the driver came to pick me up in the evening.

When I got there, there were lots of other English-speaking dancers and I saw that my fears had been unfounded. I complained to the management about the hostel, and they moved me into a house with some of the other dancers. They explained that the hostel was only supposed to be temporary as all the hotels in Vienna were full. The whole experience was a taste of how rough and ready Vienna was going to be.

I was put to work as a dancer every night at this club. It was very much like Stringfellows in the UK. It wasn't a strip club, but it was very high-end. The high-society of Germany and Austria would congregate and champagne was thousands of pounds for a bottle. During the day I'd learn the routines and practice them and then at night, we'd perform.

It was hard to fit in with the other dancers. They were cliquey and arrogant, and they found it annoying that I didn't know all of the routines. Although the money was better than I'd ever been offered before and certainly better than anywhere else, I still thought about coming home. In the end, however, I stuck at it and realised I had to prove myself to be accepted by these people. There was once a nice guy, however, called Craig. After a while, I asked him to meet me during the day so that we could practice the routines together and he gladly obliged. It took me a short time to nail it and then the other dancers gave me a little bit of a break.

I was determined to see it through. Some dancers would only last a few days before they were sent home. They couldn't cope with the culture. Most of it was driven by ego. There were a lot of beautiful people who danced at that club and the guys, in particular, did not like it if someone more built came along. There was also a lot of steroids going on and therefore, a lot of aggression. Some of the guys would snap very easily. Illegal drugs were also common. That toxic cocktail of cocaine and steroids and ego, it was all a mess.

Of course, when everyone is taking drugs to get ahead it's easy to feel the pressure that you need to join in, but I resisted. To this day I've never taken drugs. I've never wanted to let my parents down; if they thought I was involved in that lifestyle, I knew they'd be devastated after all they had done for me. That was also the first time in my life I'd been confronted with people taking drugs. At university, everyone was drinking but there were no drugs. But in Vienna in the changing room, it was like visiting a ski resort there was so much white powder flying around!

I also never quite fitted in with them because after they'd be done with work, they'd head off on a night out, burning through the cash they'd earned that night. I, on the other hand, would head home and go straight to bed. I was just there to earn money and to work my way up the ladder. I was focused. While the rest of the dancers recovered from hangovers, I'd be up early the next morning in the gym or working on my routines. Of course, I felt isolated and lonely; sometimes I felt like I worked so hard while they did nothing and would still end up more ripped than I am and find it all so easy. I reminded myself that I was doing it the hard way, without steroids.

Taking steroids and drugs in this environment had a dark side that I soon experienced first-hand. One night, I had done my usual routine of going straight to bed in the shared apartment after work, but a dancer called Christian wandered into the flat in the early hours of the morning and woke me up.

"Where is everyone?" he asked. Christian didn't live in our flat, he lived in an apartment close by with some of the other dancers as we couldn't all fit in one place. I wasn't quite sure how he got in but he kept trying to talk to me. He was a mess. He told me he'd got no money and he'd just split up with his boyfriend.

"This is not worth it," he said, reaching inside his pocket and producing three pills.

"What are you doing?" I said. I was so alarmed, but I was still half asleep.

"It's alright I've already had 7 or 8…" he said, calmly.

Now, I might not be into drugs, but I know that having 10 pills of anything is not good for someone. This was confirmed when he started laughing hysterically, running around the flat like a madman.

"Get me out of here," he screamed, and he ran into the bathroom and tried to climb down the toilet. I yanked at him, trying to pull him out. Next, he manically ran to the floor-to-ceiling-window in the bedroom, opened it and prepared to jump. I managed to restrain him. We lived high up on the fourth floor and if I'd missed him that would've been it. Without warning, his eyes started rolling backwards and he collapsed in front of me. I phone the emergency services and one of the other dancers. Rather than rushing over to the apartment, concerned about the fact that one of our troupe had potentially taken an overdose, the other dancers went mental. What I didn't know was that when you call an ambulance in Vienna, you don't just get the medics, the police always come too. I spent most of my time outside of the house training, so it had escaped my notice that the house was a drug den. There was cocaine hidden in every nook and steroids in every cranny. While Christian lay on my lap, I tried everything to get him to come around. I was in despair. The other dancers came bounding into the flat, completely ignoring Christian and hiding their stash.

They had got there just in time and managed to hide their drugs before the police arrived. The ambulance turned up and took Christian away and that was the last I ever saw of him. I have no idea what his fate was. The club called me in the next day, asked me what happened and just said they'd deal with it. Because I was on the outside of this clique due to the fact that I didn't touch drugs, I never found out even when I asked about it.

This was just one of several incidents which reveal that there was something dodgy going on at that club that I wasn't aware of. Another dancer called Jay decided to start dealing drugs himself and one day he just disappeared. He was at the club that evening. He finished his dancing and went to head out and then he just never came back. His friends packed up his belongings the next day and that was it. I never heard anything from or about him again. I have often wondered if this was because he upset the wrong person and got knocked off. There were very wealthy, powerful people who used to come to this club, no doubt members of powerful organised crime groups so this could easily have been the case.

The violence was by no means discreet either. The bouncers were heavy-duty and had no qualms about picking up a guy and ramming his head through the front door of the club because he couldn't pay the bill for his champagne.

I was never a threat to anyone. I tried very hard just to get on with things, as I'd always done, and this was my saving grace.

My life in Vienna came to an end quite abruptly after 6 months. My agent phoned me and told me about a gig they had lined up on Ant and Dec's show on ITV. The management of the club didn't want me to go, and I had to argue to get myself out of the contract. It was time for a change. I'd got enough money in the bank and I missed my mum and my dad.

Like everywhere where there's a lot of money, a lot of drugs and a lot of beautiful people, there's bound to be a dark side. London was no different from Vienna. Vienna prepared me to come back to London with my eyes open. Although I didn't know it at the time, I was about to enter the world of parties, boybands, glitz and glamour. A world heavily intertwined with the criminal underworld and the mafia.

As the plane touched down in England I felt like a new person, a suitcase full of top designer clothes with the money I'd earned and a new outlook and ready to take on the UK once more.

Craig and Glenn two good Dancer friends – Vienna

5

TELEVISION

I came back to London with a bang. I immediately got a job as a club promoter in the West End going from club-to-club on the back of an old-style Routemaster bus on a Saturday night. One night we were leaving a venue in Haymarket, I was on the mic and was entertaining everyone when suddenly the bus started to veer towards Her Majesty's Theatre where Phantom of the Opera was playing.

The girls on the lower deck of the bus started screaming. I raced towards the driver. His head had fallen backwards and he was frothing at the mouth. The bus was only going slowly but was veering straight into a theatre full of people. The driver was choking so I knew that I needed to hook his tongue out of his mouth. At the same time, the bus was getting closer and closer to the theatre. I had to stop the bus, but I also had to stop the driver from dying. I leaned over him and tried to reach the pedals but I couldn't get his feet out of the way. The handbrake wasn't working. All I could do was steer the bus away to parked traffic on the other side of the road. We hit some cars and a coach. Thankfully, no one was on board at the time. I didn't know that. It was a gamble that paid off.

As soon as the bus ground to a halt, the police and ambulance were on the scene and we managed to grab the driver out and lay him on the floor. He went to the hospital and it turns out he'd had an epileptic fit which had been triggered by the medication he'd taken.

The story was mentioned in all the papers and I felt proud of what I'd done. The owner of the bus company was a very good friend of mine and still is, so I didn't want to make too much of a big deal about it in case people thought that party busses crashing in the West End was a regular occurrence. It could have happened on any bus at any time, it was simply terrible luck that the driver had been taken ill. The incident was a reminder of the excitement I'd missed out on in London while I'd been away. There was always something crazy going on.

The main reason I'd come back was for a gig on Ant and Dec's show, the precursor to Saturday Night Takeaway. Even though it was only a small gig, it was the obvious next step in my career. It took me away from dancing, though I was still very much keen on continuing this, and it gave me a foot in the television industry.

I was involved in a sketch that Ant and Dec were doing. Dannii Minogue had been invited on as a guest and was dressed up as Cleopatra. I was dressed up as her bodyguard with no top on and had to carry her around. It was great fun and my first experience of recorded TV. It was different from being on stage where you are very much living in the moment. On TV there's a lot of waiting around and drinking coffee. I enjoyed it though because it meant more time getting to talk to people.

Compared to dancing in Vienna, it was all very nice. I think because I was doing a set role, I was treated more like 'talent' or a 'principal artist' as they call them. I spent a good two days with Ant and Dec. They were nowhere near as famous as they are now. They were exactly as you see them on TV; very bubbly and obviously real friends. Dannii was also very lovely. She had just finished filming Neighbours and was starting her own singing career. We laughed and got on very well.

Years later I went on to do Saturday Night Takeaway to film the indents for their show and they remembered me. Indents and title sequences for shows were becoming a regular gig for me. I also filmed them for Graham Norton's Show. Again, he was not as famous as he is now, and he had several late-night shows that were a little more salacious and cheekier than his current show on the BBC. We filmed at Graham's actual house. I had to sit in the bath with my top off with Graham Norton and he was sitting behind me scrubbing my back.

I spent the day with him filming and afterwards me, the

director, Graham and his boyfriend all went out for dinner. At the time he lived around Notting Hill and it was quite ordinary really. We just went to a pub and had dinner. A lot of people came up to him and shook his hand or said hello to him, but they were very good in terms of leaving him alone whilst he was at dinner and I think that might have just been because he was quite well known around the area.

I then had a brief role on The Bill. Ironically, given my experience in Vienna, I played a drug dealer. I spent a week in Wimbledon in a big house that was supposed to be my mansion and filmed loads of scenes. Eventually, as you expect in a show like The Bill, I ended up getting dragged off and nicked.

I also had a brief stint on EastEnders. I was brought in to break up Kat and Alfie who at the time were the golden couple on the square. My character met Kat at an Indian restaurant and we started talking and she ended up leaving Alfie for a bit for my character. It was a huge heartbreak, and I was all over those TV mags. How could Kat do that to Alfie? They were TV's golden couple!

Kat is played by an actress called Jessie Wallace. And she is exactly like she is in the program; very mouthy. I was trying to get one of the scenes as good as it could be, but I made a fatal error. I suggested she did something. She didn't like being told what to do by me. In her mind, I was a nobody who'd only been in EastEnders for a few days. She was quite frosty, and made a point of saying it to the director who, no doubt having heard her go off on one before, started to tease her.

"Can you stop looking at him?" the director said.

"What?" Jessie snapped back.

"You keep looking at him, focus on what you're doing."

"Ugh," she said, like a child, "I don't like him. I wouldn't look at him."

On the other hand, I got on well with Shane Richie who played Alfie. I've got quite bright white teeth and he was obsessed with them. Every chance that he got, he'd bring them up. Admittedly, I had whitened my teeth. I was approached by the celebrity dentist Larry Rosenthal who did the teeth of Catherine Zeta-Jones, Tom Cruise, Michael Douglas. He offered to do my teeth for free if I did all the modelling for his brochures. I got 30 grand's worth of work done for nothing.

Stepping into the Queen Vic for the first time was quite overwhelming. It also breaks your illusion of reality a little bit. It's a very small room. When they want to capture long shots of the whole pub they film inside a studio. If you walk around the outside of Albert Square at first glance it all looks realistic, and I thought they'd built this entire village somewhere. But on closer inspection, you realise most of the doors are just painted. You can't go inside. The experience taught me a lot about how television worked; the camera angles, how they light a stage to make it look like it's daylight outside. This role was only short-lived, and I was only in it for about a week, but it was great fun.

My next job was a presenting gig on MTV, and I had a show called 'Handy Hunks' on a channel called Live TV. It was a home maintenance show, but I had to have my top off throughout the six episodes. For example, I had to show how to put a curtain rail up. This was the early 2000s when MTV was just gathering momentum.

I was becoming a little bit stereotyped as a 'hunk' and London Tonight decided to get in on the act as well. They ran a competition, and the winner would get a grand's worth of shopping vouchers and me as their 'shopping hunk'. I would traipse around Lakeside Shopping Centre in Essex with my top off, carrying their bags for the night. There was lots of press and cameras there. I was in peak condition at that stage of my life, and I was happy to go along with it. I fitted the niche they wanted to exploit, and I enjoyed it. I look back on my life at school, where I was never the one getting the girls, and I felt proud of myself for how I'd turned things around.

These television roles, however, came to an abrupt end for a short while after one nasty incident in the gym. Spurred on to maintain the body that had allowed me to win so many roles, I was training in the gym when one of the cables in some of the equipment snapped which made the bar come down on the back of my neck. It knocked me out clean and I had to be rushed to the hospital. Even today I still have a chip in my fifth vertebra. It effectively broke my neck. It was a terrifying experience for me. I couldn't go to the gym for the next six months and I was out of action because I had to wear a neck brace. With this inactivity both physically and professionally, questions over my career lingered in my mind. In hindsight, I was very lucky. If the bar had hit my neck, even just two millimetres higher than where it had landed, it would have broken my spinal cord and I would have been in a wheelchair for the rest of my life.

I decided to sue the gym where this took place for loss of earnings. But it took two years and lawyers' fees and legal fees. It was my first experience of litigation and it was a long slog that was settled out of court for a substantial figure.

Luckily, I had not taken my eye off the ball of my interests and while my television career was building. I had also been busy working on other projects that I knew I'd be able to pick up more easily when I was fully recovered.

Thursday 1st January 1998 Advertising: Canterbury 454545 Editorial: Canterbury 767321 or Whitstable 771515 The Times 13

Times People **Times** People **Times** People **Times** People

Matt Milchard – stopped an out of control bus, whose driver was having an epileptic fit.

Model Matt hero in big bus drama

CANTERBURY model/presenter Matt Milchard found time to save a bus-load of passengers despite his busy career.

Matt, 24, is a former pupil of Simon Langton's Boys School and has recently toured as a model with *The Clothes Show's* Geoff Banks.

He has become a regular figure on cable channel Live TV, where he has done some presenting and appeared in their spoof show *Handy Hunks.*

Impressive entries in his CV include presenting a Valentines special on European MTV and dancing in a music video for hot up-and-coming star Janice Kaye.

If Janice's career takes off as impressively as it has been is tipped to, Matt has been asked to tour with her.

Recently, Matt was the object of jealousy when he did a modelling shoot with popular Page 3 babe Joanne Guest.

Matt has even been employed by Coca-Cola to deliver crates of Diet Coke to office telesales girls in an enactment of the famous TV advert.

However, it's his job as a London dancer at a West-End club that brought about the amazing events that led to him saving a bus-load of passengers.

Matt is no stranger to life-saving as he was a lifeguard at Kingsmead Swimming Pool for three years, but nothing prepared him for what was to happen to him that night.

Veering

Matt said: "I was on my way home on the bus when I suddenly noticed that it was veering all over the road. The people at the front of the bus started to panic so I tried to help."

"We were heading towards The Haymarket when I jumped into the cockpit of the bus and tried to seize control of the vehicle," he added.

As the situation grew more and more desperate Matt noticed that the driver was having an epileptic fit and was starting to swallow his tongue.

He continued: "With one hand I was stopping the driver from swallowing his tongue and with the other I was trying to steer the bus to somewhere it could be stopped."

"I decided to ram it into a some parked cars which halted the momentum of the bus and brought the trauma to an end," he concluded.

There were no severe injuries to the passengers and afterwards the driver, who was also saved, said he blacked out and couldn't remember a thing about the crash.

Away from the death-defying drama, Matt attends classes for TV presenting at the Academy of Live and Recorded Arts (ALRA). Former pupils have included Ewan McGregor.

Matt's agent used to represent Geri Halliwell (Ginger Spice) and ideally he would like to present on mad-cap shows such as The Big Breakfast and TFI Friday.

Student is top Dillon

UNIVERSITY of Kent and Canterbury student, Stuart Lambert, has won 1st prize in the Dillons Student Challenge.

The prize is a CD a week for a year and £500 in Dillons vouchers for the famous bookstore franchise.

The official presentation was held at Dillons Bookstore, Templeman Library at the University of Kent.

Stuart is currently studying English and the competition he won was part of a Dillons nationwide student campaign which included visits to over 60 Freshers' Fayres.

To win this fantastic prize Stuart had to correctly answer three questions. He successfully beat more than 5000 other entrants.

About the Bus crash…

Star Stories Channel 4 - The Krays

TV ad for 'Glist' with Julie Walters and Andy Cody

My dodgy character on 'The Bill' - James Spalding

6

OF BOYBANDS AND GANGSTERS

My few television roles had introduced and prepared me for being part of that world. Fame is a game of connections and I had learnt how to take advantage of the network that I had built up. Whilst my days were taken up with being on set and arranging my ever-expanding property empire, my evenings were soon taken over by my dancing. I did a few gigs dancing in clubs like Stringfellows and Caesars which were very similar to the club in Vienna. At Caesars customers would pay £15 for a ticket and get unlimited drinks all night. I was lowered onto the stage from a platform from above with smokes and light. It was, as you can imagine, a rowdy crowd. The bouncers at these places were top notch so we never got into any trouble. We each had a security guard standing at the bottom of our podium so no one could touch us.

I started to realise I could make quite a lot of money as a club promoter as well; I even set up my own business called Pyramid Productions with a very close friend at the time called Peter. I started building up my own guestlists and meeting celebrities that we could invite to our nights.

That period of my life was really fun. I was getting paid to meet and schmooze with all kinds of celebrities. Chris Evans and Billie Piper came down a few times, as did Atomic Kitten, Westlife, Jodie Marsh and the cast of Hollyoaks, among many others.

The promoting inevitability led to me wanting to do more than dancing. I wanted to start a pop band; it seemed like a natural progression, especially since I'd already got lots of connections from the world of television, celebrities and the nightclub scene. I linked up with two girls and another guy I'd met at Caesars. We got ourselves an agent and found some time to go to the studio and work on some songs. My good friend Ben who is a great sound-engineer/musician helped us put some tracks together and then we blagged our way onto a circuit. The tour was supposed to kick off with us performing at the opening of a big new night club in Kingston, London. There were posters of us plastered outside the club and a lot of publicity.

A couple of days, however, before this first gig, the other boy, Terry, and the girls pulled out. I was left in the lurch. It would have been so easy of me to have scarpered and just not shown up. I'm an honest person so I rang up my agent and told her what had happened. She threatened to sue me if I didn't turn up as it was her reputation on the line as well. I agreed with her that I would go on stage on my own and get two backing girls to dance behind me. I hired two girls that looked like the girls in the posters so that it looked like the band was still together and I could say the other guy was ill.

The night before the event the other girls bottled it was well; they felt under pressure and didn't have enough time to learn the routines. I rang up the agent on the night and told her what had happened again. She threatened to sue me again.

I went down to the club on the night and told the manager in person. He sent me straight to the changing room and told me I was going up on my own. What was I going to do? There is blagging it and then there is pretending to be a four-piece band on your own in front of over 1,000 people. I was mortified and going to look like an idiot. I took a deep breath, closed my eyes, momentarily and headed out to the stage.

I made up some story about the rest of the band having been in an accident or something. I was incredibly nervous, and I was just focused on trying to get through it all. The crowds seemed to love me, they cheered me and whether this was out of pity or not I don't know. By the time I finished the routine I felt a huge rush of adrenaline. I had proved to myself that I wouldn't back down in the face of adversity.

The agent was not only relieved, but she was also impressed. I hadn't let her down and that helped my reputation. Some well-known producers had heard about the incident wanted to help rebuild the band around me. They paid for auditions and before I knew it, I was back at Pineapple Dance Studios, but this time I was on the judging panel. For once I was making the decisions; the managers, the producers, the agents were all picking people they thought I would like.

After two days of auditions in which people queued around the block for a shot at being in the band, we narrowed it down to two girls and another boy to proceed with the same songs and same routines. Helen, the first girl, had long blonde hair and was very bubbly and her counterpart was Maria who had short black hair and was a bit of a diva. The guy, Danny, had come over from Marbella, where he lived and grew up. His father was a media mogul and he'd been flown in from Spain just for the audition. He had a special quality about him. He was an amazing singer, and he could sell himself. It also helped that his father was a media mogul so the other judges started to see how his father could position the band in the right magazines.

Very quickly Helen and Maria became very good friends, and I took Danny under my wing. I was 24 by this point but he was only 18. Having never lived outside of Marbella, his parents moved him over to London to begin a new life. As you can imagine it was a huge culture shock for him and I looked after him. There's no doubt he was out of his depth; he loved his home comforts and London is a totally different place from the sunny beaches and the mollycoddling family that he experienced in Spain.

I helped him find a flat. This wasn't a problem as I had quite a few houses by then and he was welcomed into a community full of other talented performers trying to make it. It was a support network which he badly needed. He felt homesick and I helped him as much as I could.

We were all quite grounded and had to spend a lot of time in the dance studios learning the routines. Danny was a talented singer, but he'd never had a dance lesson in his life, so he was slow at picking them up and started to annoy the girls. As always, I played the mediator, trying to keep the peace and help Danny get up to scratch as quickly as possible.

We started off doing a lot of studio work. We'd get put into a studio in London with a songwriter and a producer and we'd be expected to come up with some songs that we could potentially sell.

Not long afterwards we got introduced to someone keen to manage us. You need a manager who can back you because studio time is expensive. A good studio could be more than £1000 an hour. There's no guarantee at this point that you're going to get a record label interested, so it was a massive gamble.

What I wasn't aware of until I met my first music manager Joe Pyle, or Big Joe, was just how intertwined the music industry was with the London underworld or the mob.

Some powerful people pulled a lot of strings from behind the scenes. This was before people like Simon Cowell came to prominence. All the gangsters including the Kray Twins liked to have bands and celebrities around them to give them an aura of glitz and glamour, and there was a lot of money tied up in this industry. The more powerful your manager, and the stronger links they had to this world, the more sway they had with the record labels and the easier it would be for them to get you a record deal.

Big Joe was notorious. He was a nice guy to us, but he oozed power. He'd known the Kray Twins from when they were young boxers and was best man at Reggie's wedding. Later he had been put on trial for the murder of a nightclub owner for which he was acquitted in the 1960s. He was in control of a large part of London at the time. Not that I paid any attention to any of this, I just wanted to focus on the music.

We had to audition for him at his penthouse on Chelsea Harbour. It was rather like the Judge's Houses round on the X-Factor. We had to wait in a nearby café before we went to the house. The guy that met us was a huge ex-boxer called Ray. He towered over us in his smart suit. He waited for the call from them and then escorted us up into the lift. There were bodyguards everywhere; it wasn't normal. I was more used to being taken to a waiting room and given a cup of coffee in one of those plastic cups, where there might be some gold plaques on the wall, than this. We had to perform for these guys in their front room. Thankfully, we passed the test.

Once the band was in good enough shape Big Joe got us a gig at Stringfellows to showcase us. This was a big deal. Stringfellows was a major club in the West End at the time and it felt like we'd made it. I invited Jon, Garrick, my parents and my younger sister Charlotte alongside many other friends from the past. We did the gig and absolutely smashed it. It couldn't have gone better, everyone performed flawlessly, and the crowd went wild!

Afterwards in the changing rooms, Big Joe came in along with his son and his bodyguards and then all these other famous 'faces' from the underworld walked in to congratulate us. All the people that were in that room with us that night have all had books written about them. It was the elite of the London underworld, shaking my hand, hugging me and saying that I could call them if I ever needed anything. One of the reasons it was so surreal is that you would think that mixing with all of these people would be scary, but it wasn't, they were all lovely. It was very respectful.

Once I got to know Big Joe it was very obvious that he was an interesting character with a lot of influence. On some occasions, we'd be at dinners with him, and Charlie Kray would be there or one of the security guards he'd hired would have a gun visible in his pocket.

Another time I had an encounter with a gangster called

Tony Lambrianou. In the 60s, Lambrianou was one of the Kray's right-hand men who'd served fifteen years in jail for the murder of Jack "the Hat" McVitie. McVitie had allegedly been paid by Ronnie Kray to murder his enemy and ex-business partner Payne. Rather than carrying out the hit, McVitie had kept Kray's money for himself without killing anyone. Lambrianou allegedly took revenge for the Kray's and to show to the world that you couldn't get away with stealing from them.

Lambrianou beckoned me over and kissed me on the forehead. "If you ever need anything, boy,' he said, in his thick Greek accent, "you just talk to me!"

He was effectively telling me he could do favours for me if I needed to get out of a sticky situation. I wasn't naive. I knew he wasn't saying this because of who I was, it was because Joe was his boss, it was about loyalty. Not that I ever would have taken him up on his offer. I would have then owed them favours and who knows what they would have asked from me.

I never asked Big Joe about any of the people we met or involved myself with them. We were living an amazing life, drinking champagne and hanging around with other highly influential TV people. At Stringfellows on the night of our performance, Gerard Butler was sitting out our table alongside Angela Griffin, who was in Holby City at the time. All the young, upcoming stars were here networking with each other.

On another occasion, I was waiting in the green room of a recording studio and I saw a girl sitting across from us and I was convinced I went to school with her, so I went up to her and introduced myself. It turns out it was Helena Bonham Carter, not an old classmate. I felt like a complete idiot.

When you're trying to make it in this world, either as a boyband or as a TV star you have to be out meeting people all the time; it's very much a world where who you know is the most important thing.

After we had recorded a few songs, the next step was to go on tour and to get our name out there to hopefully get some interest from a record label so that we could eventually release a single. As we would soon find out, this was not as easy as we first thought it was going to be. Because we didn't have a record label and we weren't yet earning money, we were given a good wage by the management so that we could be at their beck and call. If they needed us to go on a night out to perform or impress someone, we'd have to drop everything at the drop of a hat. I really couldn't complain at this stage. I was being paid to hang out at glitzy, glamorous events and perform.

Big Joe used to organize boxing events in the West End, and we'd always get invited and left to mingle with other celebrities. We'd walk straight in, without having to pay, even though, with no record out yet, no one had a clue who we were. We even had a well-built driver who'd wear dark sunglasses to take us everywhere in a blacked-out Range Rover. On one occasion we got a phone call telling us that Joe was meeting Will Smith for dinner at Zilli Fish and we were asked whether we'd like to join them. I rushed back in the traffic to try and meet him, but we didn't make it in time, they'd left. It's always been a huge regret of mine. This is perhaps the one time I've been late to something and it's turned out for the worst rather than the best!

I put the money I was earning straight back into more houses on the street. As I got more successful, I attended more networking events and met more young talent that could make potential tenants for the houses. By the time I was 25, on paper, I was a millionaire.

My mum always tells me to stop moving the goalposts and to look at what I've achieved but I was so ambitious that there was no time for that. I was already moving onto expanding the empire and making it bigger. I suppose this is why I became so frustrated that after months with Big Joe, although I was making good money, we weren't any closer to getting the record deal that I wanted.

For a while, nothing happened on the deal front, until we were assigned to Big Joe's son. We thought he'd have the time to work with us but he appeared to drag his feet too, though it turned out he was just busy with other projects.

In April 2000, Charlie Kray died and suddenly everything was up in the air. Everyone connected to him was grieving. After a month of mourning, we still weren't getting anywhere. It was obvious there was something else going on here that we weren't privy to. It wasn't in our interests to continue as we were just treading water. I took the bold move to talk to Big Joe and his son, letting them know that things weren't working out. They appreciated this and said we could find different management if we wanted. We put some feelers out and within a few days, I get a phone call from a gruff American voice.

"Hi, is that Matt? It's Don Arden here, do you know who I am?"

"No," I said back, honestly. I didn't have a clue who that was.

"I own a label called Jet Records in the US. I've heard a lot about you, I'm going to fly over, I want to meet you." This sounded like the phone call I'd been waiting for all of my life.

"We'll meet you," I said, "whenever and wherever you want."

So once again we were back at the Judge's House. This time at plush rooftop apartment in Kensington. Surrounded by bodyguards and sat in a chair was this aged figure smoking a cigar.

Don Arden, it turns out, was a big deal. He was Sharon Osbourne's estranged father and a very influential manager in America who'd started Ozzy Osbourne's career. Because we'd kept up a good relationship with Big Joe and we'd kept out of trouble, he liked us a lot, he'd put in a good word for us with Don and now Don was happy to sign us up.

While Big Joe was tied up with the London underworld, Don was very well connected with powerful families in the US. So, although we'd moved management, we were still very much working in the less legitimate parts of the industry. The first obstacle we had to face under Don was that he wanted to get rid of Maria and Helen.

"They've got to go," he said, coldly, "It's time for some new girls."

As it happened the girls were now getting tired of it all. This had all gone on for around a year and we'd not got anywhere. So, when he let them go, they were fine about it. Arden held auditions at his house for two new girls. We were sitting on the sofa watching these girls sing and dance during the day and then in the evening he'd take us all out for dinner to discuss who was good and who wasn't.

Danny had matured by this point and knew exactly what he wanted. For him, there were no prisoners. If the girls had to go for him to get his career, then they had to go. The two girls that replaced Helen and Maria were called Tamsin and Lucinda. Tamsin was one of my tenants from one of the houses so again all of my different ventures were feeding into one another.

Finally, Arden gave us a record deal and we were back in rehearsals and the recording studio. Then one of my best friends called Andrew (AKA Supafly) joined the crew. He had previously written the songs for us at the start of things but now he was to be a full-time member of the team which Don Arden had agreed to. By this point, we were gigging, and we were getting paid good money.

It soon became clear that Don was starting to go a bit senile. He used to sit and recall stories to us about Sharon, revealing her deepest darkest secrets. He was very bitter about the fact that she no longer spoke to him. He could get quite nasty, and he was also forgetful. It was becoming a problem. One-night Don called us into his office.

"Thanks for everything guys but I've decided I'm just going to go with the girls now. Good luck. You can get your money, but it's finished now."

It was very sudden and as you can imagine me and Danny were both devastated, having put in all this work and performed all of these gigs. We finally had this big label behind us now. It seemed like we were finally about to make it and then it was like we'd had the rug pulled from under us. I was so deflated. My whole world had collapsed.

I left Don Arden's place driving away and the next day I got another shock. It wasn't enough for Don to want to ditch the girls, he wanted to keep the same music and cut us out. And he'd found a sneaky way to go about it. He approached Andrew who'd written the songs and offered him £250,000 for the rights and a publishing deal. It was a big test of our friendship but thankfully, he's above that and refused the cash. In fact, he ended up flying to Australia to chase other opportunities and get away from Don's persistence.

Don normally got whatever he wanted. To Andrew, £250,000 was a fortune. He didn't have the income from houses or other ventures like I did; I knew then he was a true friend.

If Don had taken the rights, it would have meant that I wouldn't have been able to sing my songs that I'd helped come up with. By this point, after doing gigs and schools' tours we now had a large fan base. Some young girls used to wait for us at airports. I can't imagine how weird it would have been if I couldn't perform my own songs anymore.

A couple of days later, I mentioned what had happened to us to a friend of mine called Sam. She was my dance agent and a long-time friend so of course I told her the truth about what Don had done. In the middle of the night that same day I got a phone call.

"Hi," said the familiar voice, "is that Matt?"

"Yes, hi Don, is everything ok?"

"You're playing with fire, young man." He spat.

"What?" I said, confused, and still quite groggy.

"I just had a visit." Somehow (via Sam) word had got out about what had happened, and some very influential people were not happy about it. It turns out that I had my defenders who had put Don in his place and told him off for what he'd done to me. He was not a man who was used to being told off, and he was not happy. I knew better than to intentionally start a dispute in this world.

"You don't know who you're messing with," he said, and he hung up.

The drama had done us some good because I soon got another phone call from a guy called John Coletta who wanted to take over my management. John said he'd sort out Don and presumably pay him off to smooth things over.

John was based in Marbella and had decided to fly us out. John Coletta also knew Danny's father quite well which also helped. We were on to our third manager. We could only hope there'd be no more drama and we'd stand a good shot at making it this time.

A TALE OF TWO PROMOTERS

It's easy to start a night, right? Not when the builders don't finish on time, the coach you've hired doesn't turn up and you've lost your day job. We follow two very different promoters through their first night

Mixmag write up on us as Top London Club Promoters. Myself and Peter Mikhail - Pyramid Productions

Alley Cat Dogs

Joey Pyle - Impact's first notorious Manager

Impact live show

Andrew Tumi AKA 'Supafly' has been by my side through thick and thin.

Danny and I in an early 'Impact' photoshoot

COMMERCIAL POP TOP 30

This	Last	Weeks	**ARTIST** TITLE (mixes)	Label
1	3	2	**MADONNA** HUNG UP (MIXES)	Warner Bros.
2	5	5	**DHT** LISTEN TO YOUR HEART (MIXES)	Data
3	9	4	**LEE S FEAT. DANIELLE** OPEN YOUR HEART (LEE S/HARDINO/HYPASONIC/PASCAL/FUNKY FOOKERS/STOMPIN SYSTEM MIXES)	AATW
4	2	4	**HERD & FITZ FEAT. ABIGAIL BAILEY** I JUST CAN'T GET ENOUGH (EXTENDED/FREEMASONS/RAUL RINCON/CHOSEN FEW/KENNY HAYES/ADHESIVE MIXES)	AATW
5	15	2	**EIGHT** SUPERNATURAL (ORIGINAL/XUAN/CYBORG/EIGHT FRESH/FRIDAY NIGHT POSSE/KENNY HAYES ETC MIXES)	AATW
6	N	1	**HILARY DUFF** WAKE UP (DJ KAYA MIX)	Hollywood
7	10	3	**SUNKISSED UNITED** LOVE CHANGES EVERYTHING (AURORA MIXES)	Eastern Bloc
8	N	1	**STU ALLAN** A FEELING (STU ALLEN/VISA/DJ SEDUCTION MIXES)	Power Station Recordings
9	27	2	**GIRLS ALOUD** BIOLOGY (LAMEZMA/BENITEZ MIXES)	Polydor
10	28	2	**ALLEYCAT DOGS FEAT. MC HARD KAUR** HUNG LIKE ME (MIXES)	The Lemon Group
11	11	3	**CENTS OF ENTITLEMENT** WHO DO YOU LOVE (WIP/SHARP BOYS/THE NOBODIES MIXES)	Eastern Bloc
12	1	3	**TINA COUSINS** WONDERFUL LIFE (KENNY HAYES/LEE S MIXES)	All Around The World
13	17	2	**BWO** SIXTEEN TONS OF HARDWARE (SOUNDFACTORY/JOHAN S MIXES)	Angel
14	N	1	**SUN** ENDS OF THE EARTH (TONY MORAN/SOUL SEEKERZ/JASON NEVINS/ERIC KUPPER/SOLASSO MIXES)	JH Records
15	12	5	**TOM NOVY FEAT. MICHAEL MARSHALL** YOUR BODY (TOM NOVY/ANDY VAN/MIKE DI SCALA/PAUL HARRIS MIXES)	Data
16	25	2	**SIRENS** LOVE HURTS (LOVE TO INFINITY/M*A*S*H/DODGE MIXES)	Kitchenware
17	4	4	**PARIS AVENUE FEAT. ROBIN ONE** I WANT YOU (DENIS THE MENACE & JERRY ROPERO/STELLER MIXES)	Data
18	6	4	**GEORGIE PORGIE** LOVE IS GONNA SAVE THE DAY (ADHESIVE/SOUL AVENGERZ/RIFFS & RAYS MIXES)	Adhesive/All Around The World
19	7	4	**ASWAD VS. SIMONE GIGANTE** SHINE 2005 (DJ PROM MIXES)	Gusto
20	8	3	**JAMIROQUAI** (DON'T) GIVE HATE A CHANCE (STEVE MAC/FREEMASONS MIXES)	Sony BMG
21	N	1	**SUMMER SON** SUMMER SON (KILLAHURTZ MIXES)	Gusto
22	18	2	**CHANEL** MY LIFE (HAJI & EMANUEL/GRANT NELSON MIXES)	OneTwo/Hed Kandi
23	14	4	**FREEDOM ANGEL FEAT. CHAKA DEMUS & PLIERS AND SPANN** TEASE ME (MIXES)	A.M.I.
24	N	1	**HOUSE HEADZ** STELLA (MIXES)	Nebula
25	N	1	**EURYTHMICS** I'VE GOT A LIFE (DAVID GUETTA & JOACHIM GARRAUD/SANDER KLEINENBERG MIXES)	RCA
26	N	1	**TAKE THAT** RELIGHT MY FIRE (JOEY NEGRO/ELEMENT MIXES)	Sony BMG
27	N	1	**ANDREA T. MENDOZA** CAN'T FAKE IT (ORIGINAL/MIKE DI SCALA/KURD MAVERICK/PUNKROK/KENNY HAYES MIXES)	Adhesive/AATW
28	13	4	**DE'LACY** HIDEAWAY 2005 (YOUNG PUNX/PETE GOODING/WE DELIVER/RHYTHM CODE & CHRIS LAKE ETC MIXES)	[illegible]

Alley Cat Dogs first single 'Hung Like Me' storming the charts at No.10 chasing 'Girls Aloud'...

COMMERCIAL POP TOP 30

This	Last	Weeks	ARTIST TITLE (mixes)	Label
1	15	2	**SUNFREAKZ FEAT. ANDREA BRITTON** COUNTING DOWN THE DAYS (AXWELL/FUNKAGENDA/FONZERELLI/HENRIK B/DT8 MIXES)	Positiva
2	19	2	**GWEN STEFANI** 4 IN THE MORNING (THIN WHITE DUKE MIXES)	Interscope
3	3	3	**AMERIE** TAKE CONTROL (KARMATRONIC/TRACY YOUNG MIXES)	Columbia
4	14	2	**TURBOFUNK** GOTTA MOVE (TURBOFUNK/FONZERELLI/SWEN WEBBER/AIR BUREAU/TRENT CANTRELLE & CHRIS COX MIXES)	Phonetic/Data
5	N		**CIARA** GET UP (MOTO BLANCO/DIGITAL DOG/KARDINAL BEATS MIXES)	RCA
6	9	3	**ALLEY CAT DOGS** HOW FREAKY (BASSLINERS/BLAQ MONEY/LEVAN/GAVIN KOOL/RED RHYTHM/AUDIO CAPTIONS MIXES)	Lemon
7	1	3	**BUZZ JUNKIES FEAT. ELESHA** DON'T MESS WITH MY MAN (BUZZ JUNKIES/MOTO BLANCO MIXES)	All Around The World
8	17	2	**MELANIE FLASH** HALFWAY TO HEAVEN (HANDZUP/HEADHUNTERS/GROOVE COVERAGE/FLIP & FILL/KB PROJECT MIXES)	All Around The World
9	20	2	**I AM FINN** HARD (MANHATTAN CLIQUE/FREELANCE HELLRAISER/ORIGINAL MIXES)	Ugly Truth
10	2	3	**RICHARD GREY** WARPED BASS (RICHARD GREY/SHARAM/DAVE SPOON/FILTHY RICH/SANDY VEE & FRED PELLICHERO MIXES)	Apollo
11	21	3	**LITTLE MISS ROCKER** MY BELL IS RINGING (GLOBAL DEEJAYS/JON P. DIXON MIXES)	Jamster/WAP Music
12	N		**CASCADA** A NEVER ENDING DREAM (DANCING DJS/BUZZ JUNKIES/DIGITAL DOG/FRISCO/KB PROJECT/FUGITIVE MIXES)	All Around The World
13	N		**THE SHAPESHIFTERS** PUSHER (SHAPESHIFTERS/LIFELIKE/CHUS & PENN/NIC FANCIULLI MIXES)	Positiva
14	7	4	**BOB SINCLAR & CUTEE B FEAT. GARY PINE & DOLLARMAN** SOUND OF FREEDOM (BOB SINCLAR MIXES)	Yellow/Defected
15	N		**FRUIT MACHINE** DIVA IN THE DISCO (KINKY ROLAND/GILLY BPYZ/SUNNY FUNK MIXES)	Fruit Machine
16	N		**BWO** CHARIOTS OF FIRE (RICHMANN/ORGANS WITHOUT BODIES MIXES)	Shell
17	26	2	**SALLY JAXX** SKY (DIVINE/SCOUSE IN DA HOUSE/STEVIE B/TWILIGHT MIXES)	Energise
18	10	4	**SCOOCH** FLYING THE FLAG (FOR YOU) (MILE HIGH/SILVERSTATION MIXES)	Warner Bros.
19	N		**RIHANNA FEAT. JAY-Z** UMBRELLA (SEAMUS HAJI/JODY DEN BROEDER/LINDBERGH PALACE MIXES)	Def Jam/Mercury
20	11	6	**CORENELL VS. LISA MARIE PROJECT** KEEP ON JUMPIN' (CORENELL/FONZERELL/LISA MARIE PROJECT MIXES)	Gusto
21	8	4	**SOULSEEKERZ FEAT. KATE SMITH** PARTY FOR THE WEEKEND (SOULSEEKERZ/STONEBRIDGE/DJ BOMBA/ERIC SMAX & THOMAS GOLD MIXES)	Positiva
22	13	4	**JOJO** ANYTHING (WAWA MIXES)	Mercury
23	4	4	**BLISS INC. FEAT. CARLOTTA CHADWICK** FAITH (HOXTON WHORES/7TH HEAVEN/FRIDAY NIGHT POSSE/CLUB ENFORCER/NICK SKITZ MIXES)	Lab Recordings
24	N		**ROGUE TRADERS** WAY TO GO (METRO RADIO/SUNSET STRIPPERS/MY DIGITAL ENEMY MIXES)	Ariola
25	5	4	**JAY C VS. THE ROCK STEADY CREW** HEY YOU (ORIGINAL/BEATFREAKZ/MARTIN TEN VELDEN/FRIENDLY MIXES)	Nebula
26	18	5	**CALVIN HARRIS** THE GIRLS (GROOVE ARMADA/MICKY SLIM MIXES)	Fly Eye/Columbia
27	16	6	**ALIBI VS. ROCKERFELLER** SEXUAL HEALING (FREEMASONS/BEATFREAKZ/ERICKE/DENNIS CHRISTOPHER MIXES)	Gusto
28	6	4	**SIMPLY RED** STAY	

Alley Cat Dogs 2nd single 'How Freaky' peaking at No.6

Don Arden (Sharon Osbourne's father) signed us to Jet Records

7

ON TOUR

After tidying up my life in London, I flew back to Marbella to start my new life under John Coletta's management. Coletta was a very powerful rock manager. He was responsible for launching and discovering the band Deep Purple and he was very much admired in that world; he also had history with Don Arden.

Coletta got me and Danny straight back in the recording studio. We also had a choreographer who helped us put some routines together. We'd spend the days recording and the evenings chilling on a beach. It was much more relaxed than the day-to-day grind in the hustle and bustle of London. Like Don Arden and Big Joe before him, Coletta was full of promises and grand schemes about how he wanted to scale our career. Unlike previous managers, he actually seemed to be putting his money where his mouth was. Although Coletta was more of a businessman than Don Arden or Big Joe and music was the main reason he was in the industry, I hadn't completely left the gangsters behind me. Coletta often regaled us stories from his Deep Purple days where he had to carry a gun around because all of his business transactions were done in cash. We recorded a record and then he hired a PR company in London to look after us. For the first time, we had some tours booked and a single out in Spain, though he hadn't quite managed to land another much-coveted UK record deal yet.

The PR company would fly us from Marbella to the UK every few weeks for a tour before flying us back. These tours were great fun and we shared the stage with groups like Step, Five, A1, Phats and Small and So Solid Crew. We started to get a group of loyal fans who would wait for us at the airport for autographs.

My first task, given that Danny was now able to move back in with his parents, was to sort myself out with a place to live. Coletta moved me in with a local British family temporarily whilst I looked for a suitable house.

On one memorable day the father of the family, a lovely guy, offered to drive me to the studio for rehearsals but before we went, he wanted me to go with him to meet somebody. We drove me up to the mountains of Marbella to a palatial building. A huge English man with a Northern accent opened the door and showed me around. He was topless so I couldn't help but notice the battle scars on his torso. I'd never seen anything like it. Then, after showing us around the house, he took me into his bedroom and slid back some glass panels to reveal a panic room. There were CCTV cameras, guns, samurai swords and all kinds of other crazy things. After a while, the man whisked us away. I left this house for a day at the recording studio without thinking any more about it.

Weeks later, I saw the man I was living with moping around the house, looking quite distressed.

"I need to go back up the mountains, to see him." The father said. I volunteered to go with him.

"No," he said, adamantly, "you don't need to do that." He was clearly anxious about going back there. I watched him drive off to the house in a brand-new Mercedes and come back in the back of a taxi. It turns out that the guy who'd shown me around his palatial home was one of Britain's most wanted criminals, living in exile, and the father had upset him. It was never discussed further so I never found out what had actually happened.

To me, every gangster or underworld character I met was always very polite to me. Of course, to me they weren't bad people, they were just notorious. Now and again, you'd get a small glimpse into that world and what could happen if you swayed too far away from the music. Although they had lots of money and a lifestyle, I could only imagine that there was a huge downside to that life. They were always looking over their shoulder, fearing for their life or trying to avoid getting arrested. I knew better than to dig or to ask too many questions because I knew it wouldn't end well.

Although John Coletta was more a music man, that didn't mean he wasn't just as connected, and he could do anything for me or Danny. On one occasion we heard him on the phone, which he had placed on loudspeaker deliberately for us to hear, and he began negotiating. He owned the rights to Deep Purple's songs, notably 'Smoke on the Water', and Madonna's 'Ray of Light'. The NFL wanted to play them both at the Superbowl. He negotiated a fee of $500,000 over the phone. He'd earned that money from effectively doing nothing, just from selling the rights for one night only. It was a lesson that would later come in handy when I would be faced with a decision about buying the rights to another famous artist.

Although we'd not yet got another record deal in the UK, the touring that Coletta set up for us raised our profile considerably. We would primarily do schools tours during the day, afternoon performances as a treat for some of the kids, and gigs in the evening playing some of the clubs. We would be on a tour bus for most of the time going from city-to-city, staying in different hotels. One time my mum and dad came with us as they could drive, and we didn't have a driver to take us up to Scotland. Being so busy on tour, it was nice to spend some time with them and for them to see me being successful.

A fireworks night concert at Abbey Park in Leicester was a good example of a typical event we'd do which was family orientated. We performed 'Living on a Prayer'. There was a sea of people at this event, maybe as many as 50,000 and as I sang our song, a ballad, they all got lighters or phones out of their pockets and held them above their heads, swaying from side-to-side. That moment was pure elation. As far as your eye could see people were enjoying our music, singing our songs back to us. That kind of adulation was addictive and it followed us everywhere. We'd wait around for an hour after the gig and there'd be queues of people waiting to get our autograph.

We also had a small group of ultra-loyal fans, about 5 or 6, who'd find out which hotel we were staying at or what gigs we were doing. They'd follow us everywhere. I'm still friends a few of them of them today thanks to Facebook which we didn't have back then. They were just teenage girls then but now they are grown-ups, one is a mother of two and she'll write me a message wishing me Happy Birthday.

As the tours wound down, we spent more time in Marbella than in the UK. Our record label was Mere Music, and it quickly became apparent that one of the main investors had been embezzling funds. The police were called in and all the funds were frozen. Our careers were put on pause, again, doing nothing for months on end. I used to look at some of the other bands that we went on tour with and wondered why they had it all so easy, but we were constantly up and down with these dramas that had nothing to do with us.

We waited patiently for everything to sort itself out and then 9/11 happened. The whole world went into a complete panic. My parents wanted to know that I was alright so a few days later I decided to fly back to the UK. It's hard to describe to somebody who didn't live through it just how much that one event changed everything, even though it took place thousands of miles from where I was. We know looking back that it was an isolated incident but at that time people had no idea what was going to happen. Travelling by air was now a risky affair and so too was being in a foreign country.

So, after taking off to head back to London I never went back. The label folded after the extent of the embezzlement became clear. John Coletta wasn't in touch that much; he had his own problems and perhaps 9/11 had affected his business interests. I felt very strongly that if that train wasn't going anywhere, I needed to jump off and instead focus on other prospects.

The game was also changing. As I settled back into London life people like Simon Cowell were starting to become more prominent with their shows like Pop Idol. Meanwhile, the internet was upending the power of the labels; there was so much pirating going on online that the advances were going down and down. When we started, you'd get hundreds of thousands of pounds in advances for a record deal and now the labels get nervous handing out those sums because there was no guarantee they could recoup the money.

My attention in London was turned back to my property portfolio. I realised that if I kept buying these houses on the street, I could live a great life without working too hard. So, I decided to invest much of the money I'd received from the advances from Impact back into it. Danny went off to have a brilliant solo career and I know some of the girls did quite well.

Meanwhile, I learned shortly after settling back into London life that both Don Arden and Big Joe had passed away. I was invited to Big Joe's funeral in South London. It was a huge event. They closed off most of South London and it was full of gangsters. It was like something from a film. There were people from all over the world. A well-known mafia member called Wilf Pine made a speech at the funeral and all around you could see limos. Everyone seemed to be driving the best chauffeur driven cars, all with tinted windows of course. There was a lorry full of wreaths from well-wishers and as we drove from the funeral to the wake, to which I was invited, quite an honour, there was a sea of cars, parked along the road on double yellow lines, blocking everything. Stood guarding them were well-built intimidating bodyguards that you didn't mess with. The traffic wardens milled around but all of them were too scared to do anything about it.

The funeral was a gathering of extremely powerful people, but on a personal level, it was also a symbolic end to my music career and the end of an era. These shady people no longer dominated the industry like they once had, and a new way of doing things had taken over. They were my managers, my music history and my connection to this world which, for better or for worse, had, for now, faded away.

Impact fans waiting for Danny and I at a McDonalds after a show

Alley Cat Dogs Fan Club

Alley Cat Dogs live concert

Impact on tour

8

GETTING DOWN TO BUSINESS

It didn't take long before I realised what I actually missed; touring. The adrenaline rush you get when you're travelling around, meeting different people and are performing in front of a live audience is difficult to replicate. I soon found that I had a new opportunity to do just that.

During a role I had on a Channel 4 comedy show called Star Stories where I was playing Martin Kemp, I got chatting to Neg Dupree, who was famous for his prank show Balls of Steel. The two of us got along like a house on fire and our conversation soon turned to the crazy things we'd done in our lives and the absurdity of the fact Channel 4 paid him handsomely to go around throwing burgers at people. When he suggested to me that we take some of the acts from Balls of Steel on tour and invited me to join him I couldn't resist. Our agent agreed and set it up.

I was very much the straight man to his comedic persona. We would play games with members of the audience which often descended into them throwing burgers at each other.

On one notable occasion though we went too far and one of our 'games' got us banned from the rest of the tour. We loved egging the audience on to do more outrageous things and often we'd suggest things not thinking for a moment that anyone would take us up on our offer. We suggested two audience members come on to the stage and have a race: to see who could go for a poo the fastest. Two lads came up onto the stage. There's no way they're going to do this, we thought. This was all bravado. When it came to it, they'd realise they were in the middle of a nightclub with beautiful girls and wouldn't want to embarrass themselves. One of them went for it. He dropped his trousers in front of 1,000 people. Me and Neg were speechless. Unfortunately for us, there was a relatively famous footballer in the audience at the time and he and his wife were so outraged that they got up and left. They complained to the club where we'd performed who then passed this on to the agent and we were banned from the circuit for the whole year.

Balls of Steel was, by its very nature, an outrageous show taking place in a nightclub for people over the age of eighteen. Although a guy taking a dump on stage was outrageous, the whole premise was that we were there to push the boundaries. I thought it was a bit of an overreaction to complain like that. Never-the-less we talked our way back into it after a year and did a new tour, without that particular gag. Soon, I, Neg and another guy called Tim Shaw had our prankster show on Absolute Radio every Friday at 9pm.

Russell Brand, Jodie Marsh and Tim Rice were just some of the celebrities that fell for our pranks. This little side gig was a nice way to relive the touring days later in my life.

While this was all good fun, I was determined to press ahead with my business plans. I wanted to keep growing my empire as much as I could. I always had a figure in mind of earning around £10million but I wouldn't have stopped if I'd gotten to this point. I love innovating and finding new business interests and that was always the motivation ahead of money.

Alongside the property empire which was ticking along nicely, I decided to use all of the skills and knowledge that I'd learned during my time in the band to set up my own record label. It was called Lemon Records, part of the Lemon Group as somebody had ordered a glass of lemonade during our initial meeting and the name stuck.

I got some good people around the table to help me. My old, trusted friend Andrew (Supafly) and Brian, who was a successful music manager. We decided we would manage in three genres of music that we thought were popular and would sell. One of them was a new type of music called Reggaeton, a mix of hip-hop and Latin American music that originated in Puerto Rico. We found an artist in East London and got him signed up with a deal in Miami, America. He became quite successful, and he created some great music.

We didn't just focus on finding new artists, we also got involved in buying up the rights and back catalogues to other artists. On one memorial occasion, we were sat in our offices and we got a visit from two shady businessmen from India who claimed they had hours of unheard vocals by one of the most famous singers in Asia: Nusrat Fateh Ali Khan. Originally from Pakistan, by the time of his death in 1997, he'd sold more records than Elvis and was described by LA Weekly as being the fourth greatest singer of all time. Of course, we'd never heard of him and were instantly sceptical of the Indian businessman's claims. Why, if they had this supposedly extraordinary cash cow, had they come to us? It was like two people coming up to you at the pub and mentioning that they had a Botticelli they wanted to get rid of.

At first Andrew, Brian and I all laughed at the offer. It was an opportunity however, and I decided, somewhat reluctantly, to pay to have the songs verified. We involved the lawyers, still convinced we were throwing money at a lost cause, only for it to come back as verified legitimate footage. We had indeed stumbled upon a goldmine. We claimed ownership for it and got together with a producer and put together a dubbed version of his songs, mixed with dance music and using his vocals.

Although this was well over 20 years ago, I'm still getting royalties from the songs today and they are all tied up in a new company we set up called Jelly Jam Music Publishing.

Every time one of his songs that we own the rights to are played on the radio or at festivals, we get a pay out from our publisher Westbury Music.

I have often wondered why these shady businessmen turned up at our office and didn't instead walk into Simon Cowell's office. I'm not quite sure how they acquired the tapes and I didn't think it was a good idea to ask them. If you own the original tapes and they're verified, then they're yours.

Another band we managed was called Samurai. We auditioned them, got them some studio time and then got them on TV programs like GMTV, taking advantage of my television knowledge and contacts. It was just starting to take off for them, but events soon took a turn for the worst. They did eventually go on to be quite successful and I keep up to date with their careers even though I no longer manage them.

As well as the record label we also built a very early internet platform called Lemon Auditions. This was where actors could subscribe and get live auditions emailed to them. There was nothing like that at the time, we were the pioneers of sites like that. We got my tenants, all performers, to test the site for us to tell us what features we needed to add.

Having this pool of actors and tenants that I could offer work to also came in handy when I set up Pyramid Pantomimes. Me and one of my friends Peter thought putting on pantos would be a bit of a laugh. We'd put some actors together and send them to schools and get a little bit of money for it. We started off doing 25 pantos in December one year, sending out three actors, and I then scaled it so that years later we were doing 600+ pantos each December. Peter left the UK and I bought him out of the company. Like with the houses, I had a goal to double the number of bookings for the pantos each year. It became the biggest touring panto company in the UK. We had 75 actors all doing the same show at the same time in December. Shows like Jack and the Beanstalk, Robin Hood, Aladdin and Cinderella were all very popular. The shows would rotate every year and after the fifth year, we'd start again because the school kids had left so none of them would be seeing the same show again.

In the early days, if an actor fell ill or there was a problem, I even used to partake in some of them myself. I eventually sold the company in 2019.

At the same time as I was doing the pantos, I also opened a sound and lighting company called Just Discos that's still going today with my partner Ed. On one memorable occasion, I got a phone call from the head of the UK Cub-Scouting organization and they asked me if I could handle setting up a huge event celebrating the centenary of cub-scouting. Scouts all around the country were having separate events to celebrate but they were all going to come together through big screens linking them all together.

I was asked to arrange the Nottingham Festival. So, I got everyone together in this huge field in Nottingham Forrest with 5,000 kids waiting for me to put on this huge party for them. I'd hired a disco bus, an outdoor sound rig and a DJ. Everything was ready. The stage was set.

As I made my way backstage and did the last of the preparations, I checked in with the DJ to tell him where to park and remind him of all the details.

"I hope you've got your hair done, mate," I said, "this is going out live on TV to thousands of people."

"What? I can't do that."

"What do you mean?" I said, nervously.

"I pretended I was ill at work to do the gig." It was an hour before the gig was about to start.

"Well, you'll have to wear a hat, so no one sees you."

"I can't risk it, I'm sorry."

We launched into a huge row and he then hung up and turned his phone off without warning. That was it. I was in the middle of a forest, I had no DJ and thousands of kids were starting to pile in, expecting a good time. There was only one thing I could do; it was time to launch my DJ career, live on television. Somehow, having never touched a DJ setup before in my life, I pulled it off and the party was a roaring success. I never spoke to the original DJ who bailed on me again, which was rather sad since he was a friend of mine. If I ever saw him again, I'd thank him. He launched another string on my bow of businesses.

I don't like letting people down at all. I'd rather do it and go through with whatever stress it may cause me than ever let anyone down. My biggest driving factor is that I don't just like to talk the talk, I think it is important to walk the walk as well. I'm always down for helping people with their ideas but at the end of the day if you don't do something then someone else will get in there and do the same thing. If I have an idea, I will go for it. I believe that anything is possible if you put your mind to it, that's my motto in life. My close friends love taking the mickey out of me for this. I'll be at a bar telling people about an idea and then the next moment I would have launched it. Always give it a go. With hindsight, I would say I jump in too quickly to things. Dive in first, learn to swim later!

I'm also not great at delegating. I like to do everything myself including managing my property empire which led to lots of work on my part. I had people who owed me rent who would disappear overnight but because I had a personal relationship with many of tenants, some of whom I'd consider friends, we often nipped this in the bud early. There would often be a phone call in the middle of the night letting me know that someone was packing their bags and moving out. I'd rush around there and catch them, ensuring they paid their rent before they left.

I have had some less favourable tenants in my time, some have caused trouble for the other tenants. I'd always go to the house to try to mediate. On one occasion a tenant who'd flouted their final warning for having a drinking problem had come back drunk with an air rifle and was shooting cans in the back garden from his bedroom window. One of the neighbours called the police who escalated it to the armed response team. By now, after the incident with the replica cop gun in McDonald's, I was used to seeing them.

I also had an older tenant who died. Every time I went around to the property, he'd give me lots of excuses about why he couldn't pay the rent or why I couldn't go into his room. When he died, I had to break down the door and what I found was truly crazy; he'd been living like a hoarder, the room was more like a tropical jungle than a place where a tenant had lived. There were towering plants everywhere, old clothes, food that had been put to one side for months on end.

I felt at the time that if I hired an agent, they would have taken 10-12% and left everyone to their own devices so it wouldn't have given me an easier life. Everything would have imploded, and it was better to be hands-on. As I would shortly come to find out, handling everything myself meant I was indispensable and if I ever got into any trouble the whole thing could come tumbling down. I was prepared to take on the added stress and to keep the extra money. There's no doubt that if I were doing it all again, I'd have an agent straight away. I've learned my lesson.

I never really thought about the stress or the late nights, it just seemed easier to handle everything myself. Looking back at the number of projects I was taking on, I felt that my body was about to burst; undoubtedly, I was burned out.

By the time I'd reached the ripe old age of 29, I was at the pinnacle of everything. I was a wealthy man; I'd just bought a brand-new Mercedes convertible, lived in a 3-bed Docklands apartment overlooking the Thames and had a large property portfolio and numerous other successful businesses. I had achieved my dream goal of being in a boyband as well as various short television appearances and roles. Looking back, it's safe to say that I had achieved more in my 20s than most people do in their whole lives.

Modelling shoot for Burberry

Photoshoot for All Saints

Myself and Charlotte

Modelling Shoot for Shell Garages nationwide

Best of friends 'Joey & Christina Wedding'. From left; Louise, Garrick, Me, Christina, Joey, Jon, Pete and Ben

BLITZ

9

THAT BLOODY STEAK

After working hard for so long I decided to fly to Marbella to have some chill time with my friends from my time there. It was the first time I'd had to properly relax and reflect on my various successes. I spent some time with Danny and some other ex-bandmates. On the last day before he drove me back to the airport, we had a farewell meal at a restaurant in Puerto Banús overlooking the harbour. It was a pizza restaurant but for some reason, I decided I wanted a steak. As I sat looking out at all the yachts in the marina, I bit into the steak. It wasn't very cooked at all. It was horrible so I left half of it. Danny joked that he hoped it didn't give me food poisoning. I finished eating and Danny dropped me at the airport. I flew home with no problems.

The following day I was due to go to Lady's Day at Ascot. I hired a classic morning suit with top hat and tails, and had a car take me to the Hilton Metropole on Park Lane to meet the rest of the group I was going with.

I suddenly felt ill. I had terrible pains in my stomach. I phoned my dad because my parents are always my first port of call.

"I feel awful," I said, from the toilet where I was hiding. He advised me to get a cab home since I wasn't going to enjoy the day anyway. I went straight to bed.

When I got up the next day, I felt ok again, though of course I was slightly gutted that I'd wasted all that money. I got on with the day's events. I went to a modelling job in Richmond but during the shoot, I suddenly lost the ability to speak coherently. I didn't realise what was going on; my tongue was paralysed. The photographers thought I was messing around with them, but I wasn't. I told them this was serious, but I couldn't get my message across.

After a while, the director started to get annoyed with me; this wasn't a joke anymore, my 'playing around' was starting to irritate him. Then my eyes started to slip. I couldn't keep them open. I walked out of the shoot, much to the displeasure of the casting director, and got a cab home. I told my dad, as best as I could, and he said he'd meet me there.

I opened the front door after a stressful journey back through London, trying to physically hold my own eyes open, but as soon as I stepped over the threshold everything went black...

When my Dad found me collapsed in my apartment, after rushing to my place from Kent, my face had dropped on one side. I looked as if I'd had a stroke, which was unheard of for a twenty-nine-year-old. He called an ambulance and I was rushed through London with the blues and twos blaring out around me.

I can remember the ambulance journey and getting to the hospital. They were trying to get to the bottom of what was wrong with me, but I still couldn't talk. I was getting unbelievably frustrated. After a while, they gave me some water to drink but every time, I swallowed it, it blew straight out of my nose. That was when things got really serious. My windpipe was closing. I don't remember anything after that.

I had dropped into a coma, having had a tracheostomy, on a life support machine. I was in intensive care for about three weeks.

Although I was in a coma, medically, I was still awake. I was on so much morphine that I still don't know whether the experiences I had were real or it was the drugs. I could hear what was going on around me, but I was paralysed. My eyes were taped shut so I couldn't physically see what was happening. My eyes weren't lubricating properly as I was unable to blink so I had to have them sealed shut. The doctors would come around every hour put some eye drops in and shut them again to keep them hydrated.

I was also hallucinating quite a lot; I felt awake. I was convinced that there were ghost children all around me, all dressed in Victorian clothing trying to play. It scared the hell out of me. I was just lying there and there was nothing

I could do about it. On another occasion, I felt the window was open and that snow was coming in and falling on me. Once again, all the nurses were dressed up in Victorian style clothes. One time I was lying on a cart and in the distance, I could hear a bell ringing as someone bellowed 'Bring out your dead.' It all felt so real; I was living through it. I had no way of waking up from these scenarios. The terror it caused me was absolutely real, and though logically, it was clearly a hallucination, there was something very literal about the experience. It felt very real to me.

During my time in intensive care, my parents stayed by my side and kept trying to call me back. They all knew I was there, and I could hear them, but I couldn't respond to them. One time I could hear them all crying around me, and I felt like I had a choice. Either I just relaxed and passed away, or I fought back. I came back, and I survived. Everything went white, as they say, it does. Medically this is due to a chemical reaction when your brain is starved of oxygen as it prepares to shut down. I focused on a picture of my family in my mind and thought of them. I don't want to do this I thought, I have to hang on for their sake and they resuscitated me. I came back.

Weeks into me being in a coma, having already been resuscitated once and having been given a blood transfusion, the doctors still had no idea what was wrong with me. I was given every test and procedure known to man including dialysis which was desperately needed.

They were also flying specialists out from all over the world to try to figure out what had happened. A retired doctor at the hospital remembered dealing with a similar case, 40 years ago in London. He came out of retirement to see if he could figure out what was wrong with me. He suspected that I had botulism and he wanted me tested for it.

Botulism is a rare disease and it's largely been eradicated in the western world. According to the World Health Organisation it is a 'serious, potentially fatal disease, which is caused by the ingestion of potent neurotoxins... formed in contaminated foods. In the absence of oxygen, the spores of the Clostridium Botulinum bacteria... excrete toxins. They are ingested through improperly processed food in which the bacteria or the spores survive...' In layman's terms, it was a rare type of food poisoning that produced toxins so powerful they could attack the nervous system and close down the whole body if it wasn't treated quickly.

The diagnosis was exactly right. I'd eaten this poison in its rawest form in the steak in Marbella. It had gone into my bloodstream and then been absorbed into my stomach which is why I just had a stomach bug when I was supposed to be at Ascot. Meanwhile, it was working its way up the bloodstream and towards my brain which is when I started to have really serious problems. The poison also set off a chain reaction which led to me contracting Guillain-Barré Syndrome, in which the immune system starts attacking itself and it further damages the nerves. To make matters worse the variant I had contracted, the 'Miller Fisher' variant, is the most dangerous as it attacks the brain first.

I was told that this was the first case of botulism in the UK in 40 years. I was so lucky that the one doctor who knew about this had only just retired from the Royal London Hospital in Whitechapel that I'd been admitted to.

When someone is diagnosed with botulism it's classed as a public health emergency, it's a big deal and the source of it has to be thoroughly investigated to prevent any future outbreaks. Environmental health officials first went to my apartment and took all food contents out for testing, thinking at first that it could have come from a tin can; you're susceptible to it if you eat baked beans out of a tin can. They then flew over to Marbella to investigate the restaurant as well. This is where they suspect I picked up the toxins. Because I'd ordered a steak at a pizza restaurant, an unusual order, the chefs had probably found a piece of steak in the freezer that had been lying around for years and decided to cook it.

After my diagnosis, doctors discovered that I had some movement in my right. My family had this idea that they could get me a whiteboard so that I could communicate with them. I would write to them, though of course, I couldn't see what I was writing so I had no idea if what I scribbled was legible. That was a turning point at which I began a very slow recovery.

Once I could communicate the doctors got in there

straight away and tried to get some answers from me about what had happened and what I'd eaten in the days leading up to my complete collapse.

Another big problem I had was my weight. I had so many issues and I was paralysed that I was having trouble eating. I had to have a stomach peg. This where the doctors drill into your stomach and insert a tube so that you can have food and nutrients pumped directly into you. It was another major operation. By this point, some of my feelings had started to return. They hadn't given me enough anaesthetic so I could feel this burning in my stomach as they went to put it in the tube, and I could smell it too. It was agony. All I could do, with only my arm fully functional and unable to communicate, was to slap the doctor as hard as I could. Only then did they realise what was happening and injected loads more anaesthetic to numb it before continuing. It was like something from a horror movie.

I was, by this stage, a total mess. My weight had plummeted by over half to a skeletal six stone, I had a stomach peg hanging out of me, a tracheotomy because I couldn't breathe unassisted, and my eyes were taped shut because I couldn't blink of my own free will. However, with the small movement in my right arm and a clear diagnosis, I was able to be moved out of intensive care and into a private room to begin my recovery. My mum moved in next to my hospital bed so she could keep an eye on me while my Dad moved into my apartment so they could be with me every single day. My sister also had a neighbouring apartment in Docklands.

The road to recovery was a long one and I had several setbacks. First of all, I contracted MRSA, the superbug which was a big thing at the time which was doing the rounds. I had to be quarantined in a separate room and everyone had to wear gowns and facemasks before they could come near me. Two of my best friends lived abroad at the time. Garrick, from my school days, flew from New York to see me and he wasn't even able to come into my hospital room. He just had to stand behind a window looking at me in sheer disbelief.

I also had a serious issue with one of the agency nurses who almost killed me. While I couldn't see anything because my eyes were taped shut, I could hear clearly. My sister, Charlotte, had bought me a television for my room. One evening EastEnders was on and an agency nurse had come to clean the mucus from my tracheotomy which builds up in your throat. To get rid of it a nurse has to put a sort of vacuum cleaner inside of your tube to clean it, it's not the nicest of procedures. As she's doing it, she's too focused on EastEnders and she starts to choke me. My mum and Dad had gone off to get some food just for a moment, thinking I was safely being looked after by the nurse. They came back just in the nick of time and managed to pull the vacuum cleaner out of my throat. Both my parents are calm people, but I can distinctly remember my Dad screaming at the nurse and straight away had her thrown out of the room. My parents made sure to make a formal complaint about her.

It was three months before I could leave the hospital. Every week they'd promise I could leave but every week they'd decide I wasn't up to it. Eventually, they let me go back to my apartment in London. That was the first step.

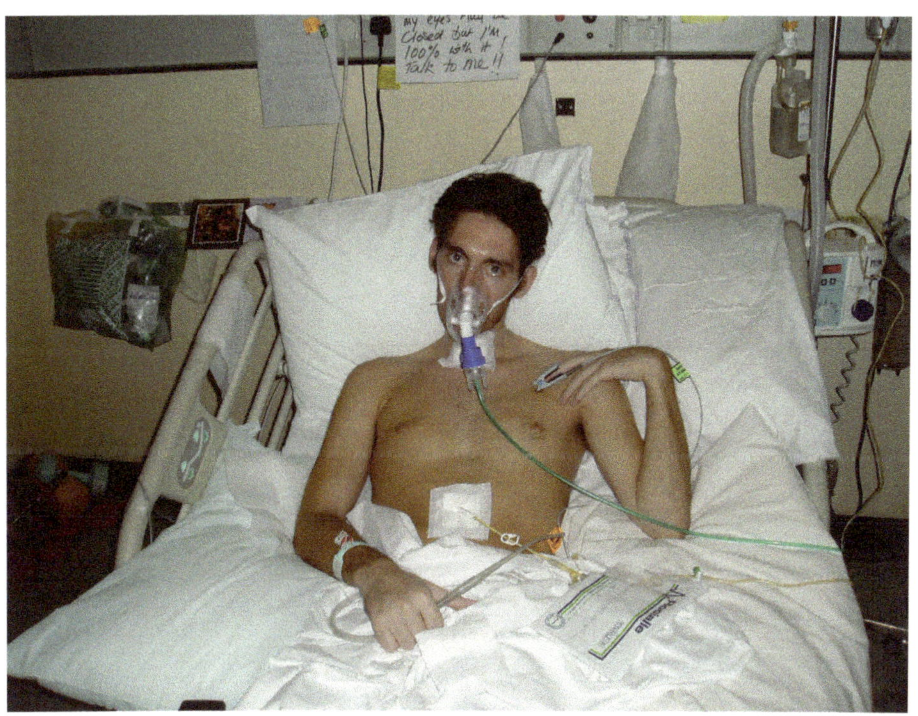

On the way to recovery

10

LIKE A PHOENIX FROM THE ASHES

As I got more conscious, I realised that, whilst in the hospital, my life had rapidly fallen apart around me. Many of my tenants had stopped paying rent, putting my property empire in jeopardy. I also wanted to continue with my acting and modelling, but I'd lost a lot of weight and wasn't physically up to it. I wanted so desperately to get back to normal that it spurred me on to recover.

When I was still in hospital my mate sneaked in some dumbbells for me which I kept under the bed. I'd be standing up like a skeleton trying to do some small bit of exercise. I was trying to push myself to get fitter quicker. This was against the doctors' orders.

By the time I was discharged and sent home I'd had the tracheostomy taken out so I could breathe on my own, but I still had the stomach peg in. Walking on my own was still a huge challenge, I'd have to hold onto a rail or the wall to manage it. I also had to take a load of equipment back with me. At night-time, I'd have to plug myself into a machine to keep me hydrated. My parents also had to move in with me as I wasn't capable of fully looking after myself.

For someone so used to an active lifestyle and all the glamour of the music industry, it was a shock to the system. Suddenly I couldn't leave the house anymore and my world was very small. The doctors warned me that it would take several years for the nerves to rebuild themselves. It could be a while before I was even able to walk again. I was not happy about that. I was determined to get back to normal as soon as possible. I set about trying to recover. When my mum wasn't watching I'd go into the kitchen, secretly make myself a protein shake and inject it into my stomach peg so that I'd have the energy to work out and put some weight back on.

Gradually as I got more mobile the exercising at home turned into going to the gym and the swimming pool. I was lucky that beneath my apartment in Docklands was a 24/7 complex. I used to wait until the middle of the night, sneak down there with a hoody on so nobody could see me or my skeletal body, that I was frankly ashamed of, and work hard on building myself back up, bit by bit. I covered the stomach peg up with waterproof tape and put on a t-shirt while I swam so no one could see it if someone happened to come down in the middle of the night.

I made a lot of progress, but I also had setbacks, moments where I felt I'd never get better. Being largely confined to my apartment my day consisted of watching a lot of TV and one time I had to ring Sky to find out why my box wasn't working. They couldn't understand what I was asking because my speech was so slurred; the operator thought I was making a prank call and hung up. This did little to boost my confidence or state of mind. I lived like this for six months.

Meanwhile, unbeknownst to me, my family had stepped in to take over my businesses for me. My sister took over the running of my panto company and being a successful actress, she knew exactly what to do. My Dad took over the running of my houses, but it was quite a challenge for him. He was connected with them, anyway, having put up some of the money in but he had no idea who owed rent and all the mortgages were coming out of my account. He had to get on top of it very quickly. In between his work and tending to me, he'd be back and forth between all the houses chasing tenants for rent and overseeing any maintenance that needed doing.

Without me there to smooth it all over, tenants now felt they could get away without paying rent, lying to us, and disappearing without notice. It was such a mess but I'm so grateful to my Dad because he covered the mortgages for me to keep it all afloat.

At that time though I was just focused on recovery and wasn't made aware of the difficulties, which I'm grateful for. As I continued to improve physically, the next step was to have speech therapy. The speech therapist decided the best way forward was for me to sing as much as I could. So, we set up a karaoke machine in my front room, much to the displeasure of my neighbours. Since my tongue was still paralysed my singing must have sounded awful.

Gradually I started to venture out of the house more and my parents started to only spend a few nights a week at my apartment. Before long I'd be at the gym every morning, pumping iron and getting myself back in shape.

I remember the time when I was able to eat and drink for the first time. I really missed coffee. I took the first sip in months and it was pure elation, though it didn't feel or taste the same as it once had. I had unfortunately lost my sense of smell and taste and that would take years to come back to me. Even now my taste and smell are not quite right. The elation stemmed from the achievement and the feeling, knowing it was inside of me and that I'd drank the first normal drink; my recovery was in full swing.

With my finances in disarray because of the situation with the houses and owing my Dad a lot of money, I was desperate to get back to work as soon as possible. My partners had taken over the running of Lemon Records, though we did lose the girl band because I was their direct manager.

Now the shoe was on the other foot. I could see it from their perspective having become frustrated at not getting anywhere when I was managed by Big Joe and Don Arden. The girl band were keen to develop their dreams and so it probably was in their best interests to do so.

The loss of the girl band and my time lying in bed had given me pause for thought. I wanted another stab at making it in the music industry because being on tour had been one of the best times of my life. I was older though, and most would have said too old to start a new band. I was determined to try again. Setting myself this goal spurred me on with my recovery. I went back to Pineapple Dance Studios at Covent Garden and rehearsed with dancers that were ten years younger than me.

Very serendipitously, while I was rehearsing at Pineapple, I had a phone call from Andrew, my loyal friend and songwriter. After a brief stint in Australia where he'd become quite successful, he was now back in the UK.

"Matt," he said, knowing that I wanted a project to get my teeth into, "I've got an idea for you. We're going to do an answer back to The Pussycat Dolls," They were big and storming the charts at that time. Their song, 'Don't you Wish Your Girlfriend Was Hot Like Me,' was everywhere at that time.

His idea was that we'd put together a 'man band' called the Alley Cat Dogs around me and we'd have a song called 'Don't You Wish Your Boyfriend was Hung like Me.'

My eyes lit up; this was my way back in. In a few short weeks after auditioning people from all over the country at Pineapple Studio, we were in the studio recording the song with a brand-new band. We got a deal very quickly.

This was the first time I got a CD in the UK. With Impact,

we'd only ever had a single out in Spain and the rest of Europe. But the Alley Cat Dogs made it to the UK. A proud moment. We released the song at the same time as The Pussycat Dolls were in the charts which gave us notoriety and we got to number 7.

On a couple of times on various TV shows, The Pussycat Dolls were questioned in interviews about us which helped boost our profile. Sadly, we never got to meet them. Our songs were also played in the Big Brother house and from the back of all of that we set up another tour.

Ten years later after I had left the industry, I was back doing what I loved. I was a lot more in control this time. My experience with Lemon Records had taught me a great deal. I wasn't relying on other people, I felt as if I had a hold of the steering wheel this time around.

For two or three nights a week, we'd be doing gigs in nightclubs around the country, and then we'd be back on our tour bus, laughing as we went. We'd get to the club and be treated well, usually being offered a free bar after we'd done our shows. The band members were all my age and we started something as many groups that followed after us were all slightly older 'man-bands'. We'd do shows with groups like Blue and also The Dreamboys.

Some of our later songs were quite raunchy with the idea that they'd appeal to older women, so it was very much an adult theme whereas before we'd been used to playing schools and family-friendly venues.

As we went along and our popularity grew the management decided to change the line-up and they got rid of two of the guys, feeling that the dynamics were wrong. They kept me on though. After then things got slick and they toned down the raunchiness of the act, so we were able to do venues like Butlins and holiday camps.

During my hospitalisation doctors had warned my family that the illness might have permanently damaged my voice box and I might not ever be able to talk, let along sing again. Yet here I was on tour with my band, making waves. I felt like I was a phoenix rising from the ashes, reborn after my illness. Whilst in hospital, my parents put a poster of Impact across from my bed so when I could eventually see, every day I would sit up and draw inspiration from myself. I was going to sing again and now, less than a year later, I'd done it. It was a huge achievement. I'd defied all of the odds.

Going on tour with the Alley Cat Dolls made me realise what I wanted to spend my time doing. The houses, great whilst they lasted, were now causing me quite a bit of stress. They were the one part of my businesses where I owed my dad quite a bit of money. I kept them stringing along, taking in regular money, but one incident in particular made me realise that I should move away from the property business. It was time to cash out. A particularly bad tenant refused to pay rent and after exhausting every other avenue, I took him to the small claims court to demand my money back. He lied through his teeth but thankfully the judge saw through it and awarded me a judgement for the sum of the rent. Unfortunately, that wasn't the end of it. Although I won the court case the tenant and his dad decided to get revenge. They rang environmental health and accused me of being a bad landlord; bullying tenants, locking fire doors, a host of false allegations, just to get me into as much trouble as they could. Although the allegations couldn't be proved they did trigger an environmental health inspection and during it, they realised that many of my houses did not conform to new regulatory standards that had just been introduced.

The House Act 2004 increased the regulation of what are known as Houses of Multiple Occupation (HMOs). These were houses where the tenants were from different households, they weren't all one family but they lived in one house, renting the rooms separately. It was supposed to stop dodgy rogue landlords from filling up their rental houses with 20 tenants and charging them to stay in squalid conditions. Because my rooms were all rented separately, I fell into that category. Environmental health wanted over £100,000 of improvements to bring the houses up to the new standards. Every bedroom had to have a separate sink and the rooms had to be a certain dimension. This meant that I had to convert some of the smaller rooms into larger rooms meaning that someone had to lose out on their tenancy.

All of my houses were brand new three-storey houses in the centre of London. This wasn't a Victorian slum. Because of these new regulations, I had to turn them into places that were more like hostels. To me this level of regulation was ridiculous. My tenants, all young actors, were all happy with the houses beforehand and now they all had to be asked to leave while I carried out the work at my expense and when and if they came back, they would be less luxurious than they were before. It seemed to be a sign of the times, so I decided to gradually sell them and to move on.

It meant was that I now had money to play with to invest in other businesses. I had all sorts of ideas that I wanted to get into. I still had the panto company which was running successfully, but that had the inherent problem of being completely seasonal. For ten or eleven months of the year I had a huge wardrobe of outfits and equipment in storage just lying around; there was surely a way of putting this to use and making some money. Soon enough I realised I could set up a children's party business.

I used the same props that I already owned and set up Just Kids Parties, we'd do private birthday parties and then some huge corporate companies who wanted us to run their annual Christmas parties for the children of staff. We often turn their whole offices into a winter wonderland for them with a Santa's Grotto and all the trimmings.

During the year we'd do kids' parties in people's gardens. Being based in London some of our clients were very wealthy and had high expectations. One parent wanted all the kids to have an iPad in their party bag. There was serious money at stake but of course, often what you'd find is that the parties weren't for the kids but were a competition for the parents, seeing who could outdo everyone else in the neighbourhood. Like the panto business, we scaled this pretty quickly and in no time at all, we were doing 30 parties every weekend and I employed a whole team.

At one party, in particular, my entertainer had dropped out at the last moment. This was a kid's garden party in Wimbledon in a huge posh house. I jumped in my car, dressed up as a cowboy, picked up a party kit from the office on the way, and set off to do the party myself. How hard could it be, right?

I turned up and the mum introduced herself, leading me into her back garden which had been set up like a movie set from a western film. There were these huge hay bales and a stage set up ready for a performance. As the parents started arriving, they also sat down on the hay bales looking toward the stage.

"So," she said, "what time's the puppet show starting?"

I'd never done a puppet show in my life. I didn't even have any puppets! I eventually had to tell the mother that the office hadn't informed me about the puppet show and had to borrow the puppets from the mother herself. I just had to get on with it with the tools at hand. I went behind the stage, doing this god-awful puppet show, cringing and wanting the whole world to swallow me up. I knew the kids would be ok with it, but the parents would be mortified. It was truly terrible. I finished up with it as soon as I could and tried to move on quickly, distracting the kids with cake and other antics. The mums looked horrified.

I did my very best to salvage the mess that I'd found myself in but the mum who'd booked it was not happy at all. I felt so humiliated. I couldn't go and ask for money and as I left, she confronted me and told me clearly that she wouldn't pay me. I was just glad to get out of there in one piece; it was the party from hell.

It was around this time when a night out at an exclusive party in Chelsea led to me forming yet another unlikely lifelong bond and yet another business venture which is still going strong today. I was there with a girlfriend at the time. In our drunken state we got into a horrific argument over something insignificant. Her best friend, who was also drunk, jumped on the bandwagon and I told her to mind her own business. Somehow, this then escalated to a tussle with her boyfriend! Someone has the common sense to pull us apart and later on I found out that he happened to be an ex-world champion kickboxer. It would have been one hell of a fight.

A few days later we happened to be walking in Greenwich and we bumped into the two of them again. At first, we gave each other the 'death stare' then agreed that the four of us should go into Costa Coffee and clear the air. After a while it soon became clear we had a mutual interest in martial arts and happened to know a lot of the same people. We soon put our differences aside and Jamie and I became close friends.

Together, we founded Pyramid Martial Arts. We have remained the best of friends throughout the years and have embarked on many an adventure together. We are still very close. PMA now has five gyms dotted around the country with over 1000 students enrolled. We also had the honour of hosting the London Open 2019 which attracted over 800 fighters from around the world.

Another random business venture I invested in was having a Santa sleigh built, again with Jamie (as well as a talented fighter he has an incredible flair for design) , that could legally drive on the road. After setting up Just Kids Parties, I was thinking a lot about what kids might like. There wasn't a real-life sleigh that could be driven on the road anywhere. So, I bought a milk float and commissioned Jamie to help transform it into a roadworthy sleigh. It got quite a lot of notoriety. I was able to use my television connections to rent it out for various TV programs and adverts.

We had celebrities wanting to hire it out. On one notable occasion, I drove around London dressed up as Santa with Vern Troyer, Mini-Me from Austin Powers, in the back of the sleigh dressed as an elf. We drove around London trying to get a parking ticket as a publicity stunt; wouldn't it make for a great story to sell to the papers about Father Christmas and his elves getting a parking ticket?

The paparazzi were fully on board, but the council realised it was a setup. They knew it would cause bad publicity for them so they radioed all of the attendants and told them not to play ball. We'd park up somewhere, traffic wardens would clock the sleigh, hang around it but not give it a ticket! One of them told us what had happened, and we gave up. We still got a few good stories out of it in the papers. Another year I was tasked with picking up Katie Price and her family for her reality show. I drove them around their village in it dressed as Santa. It has since been used on This Morning and many other TV shows as it is truly one of a kind.

My experience running kids' parties was certainty a big departure from being in a band and managing rental houses, I now had a lot more people working for me.

Training Oliver to be a champion from the age of one

Winning the Freestyle Kickboxing British Championships 2017.

Myself, Cousin Amy and Mum

Corporate Xmas events organised by Just Kids Parties

Laura - my partner and mother to my beautiful children

Laura and I when we first got together.

Driving around the West End of London in my Custom-Built Sleigh with A-list Verne Troyer. trying to get a parking ticket

Oliver and I on one of our most amazing, memorable holidays. Disney Caribbean Island while on the Disney Cruise.

11

THE GIFT OF GIVING

While I've always been a keen businessperson with huge ambition, I've never lost sight of the fact that other people are less fortunate than me. I've always wanted to give something back.

One of my very close friends Oliver, who used to visit me regularly in the hospital, had a business idea that I thought would be a lot of fun and would enable us to literarily give money away for free. The idea was that we'd go around the world, handing out money dressed up as Robin Hood.

Oliver's main mission in life is to bring love and happiness to the world and he'd talked about this for ages. I said to him, "enough talking, let's just do this."

Since we had a huge array of costumes from my kids' party business in storage, we already had Robin Hood costumes. The most obvious place for us to attract the most publicity was in New York. This was a place I was familiar with. Garrick from my school days lived there and I'd once met Andrew, my business partner at Lemon Records, for a memorable breakfast here. He invited one of the wealthiest people in the world who'd just bought a skyscraper for over $1billion to join us. New York is a city where dreams are made, for me, everything was possible there.

We hopped on a plane and headed stateside. We withdrew $10,000 and had it all changed up into $1 bills. We created a website, Olivier's idea, for ourselves which would give hints about our next location around the world and people would be able to follow us. We'd make money by selling the advertising space. We stapled a business card promoting the brand and the website to each bill and we set off. We informed the paparazzi in advance, provided we got a cut of the sales of the photos to newspapers. We'd then put this money towards our next giveaway.

We dressed up and started giving handfuls of dollars away to people who held the doors open for us and to homeless people. I had the megaphone to tell people around us what was going on and another one of our team had a secret camera recording people's reaction. Many people initially turned us away, not accepting or believing us. It was a nice feeling knowing we were giving something back.

We were all buzzed. On the second day, we courted the press and went to Washington Square Park with huge bags of cash between us. We threw a cloud of dollar bills into the air. People were slightly nervous at first and didn't know what to make of it and then they started laughing and screaming.

By the time we'd ran out of money people didn't believe us and started chasing us. We had to disappear.

When I got back to my hotel room my phone rang. It was my Dad, asking if I was alright, bearing in mind that none of us had told anyone what we were doing, and our masks disguised our identity.

"I heard Robin Hood is with you," he said.

It turns out that just 30 minutes after we'd got back to the hotel, we'd appeared as the top story on the six o'clock news back in the UK. The next day we were on page 2 of The New York Times and it was soon picked up in Australia and all over the world. Getting the paparazzi there had been a smart idea. As soon we got off the plane in London we went straight to the office of the now-disgraced celebrity publicist Max Clifford; at the time he was the one man in London who could be sure to get you fame and fortune.

Sadly, although the idea was great it didn't go much further. Whilst we did loads of interviews, one of the Robin Hood team members started promising money to every charity he could. We had all agreed to keep it anonymous, but he decided he wanted the publicity for himself; he told everyone who would listen that he was involved in it to get himself famous and pull girls. We couldn't possibly commit to the sums he had promised to different charities, and he kept on doing it, no matter how many times Oliver and I told him to stop. In the end, we had no choice but to close it all down. Neither of us have spoken to him since. But it remains an amazing memory.

I am proud to have been involved in so many different and interesting business. A few years ago, I co-founded 'Under One Roof' with two friends, Laura and Anne-Marie. This is a chain of children's centres including soft play, a nursery, a café, a children's shopping village, fitness and dance studios and even a theatre all 'Under One Roof'. We now have venues in London, Ramsgate and even Bulgaria and are currently looking for other opportunities across the globe. We are also partners in Dinky Town, a partnership with my sister-in-law. We created a miniature village where children can dress up and role play as anything that they can imagine!

Enchanted Kingdom is another venture I am particularly fond of. Created by myself, my partner Laura and her sister Katie, a very special party venue designed to capture the imagination of every young visitor. I got some of the top designers from Chessington World of Adventures and Universal Studios to create a miniature 'Disneyland' style venue with multiple rooms that be hired out for kids' parties. I have also created Xmas World with two close friends Zahra and Parisa (also now partners in Under One Roof) in which we build magical winter wonderland villages for children and families at Christmas time each year. The famous sleigh that I rode around London with Mini-Me also makes an appearance each year.

I also have a concierge business called Pure Opulence. Given the number of contacts I've made over the years, I soon realised that I could source hard to get things or arrange amazing once-in-a-lifetime experiences for other people with just a few short phone calls. If you want to fly your fiancé out to South Africa on a private jet to see the diamonds for her engagement ring being dug out from the actual mine itself and cut, I can make it happen. If you want the rarest Airfix model kits that are sold out across the country to appear in your child's party bags for a special birthday, I've got your back. If you want to get into the most exclusive parties in the world and need a guest list, let me know, I'm still owed a few favours.

For many years after my illness and recovery, I was so focused on all these businesses that I had little time to focus on developing a relationship. None of them seemed to stick. It was only as I got older and I settled into my businesses, making them more secure, that I met someone right for me. Someone who fits into my life and shares my passion for business and success.

Laura was running a shot-girl agency called Revolver and I needed some exclusive help for an event I was running. I employed her company to do my events for me and we got on very well. She then invested in Just Kids Parties and became a partner in more ways than one. I returned the favour by becoming a partner in Revolver too, which later became Urban Angels. Together we grew this business bigger and more quickly than we could have on our own. We operated at 10 of the most popular nightclubs in the West End of London; places like Zoo Bar, Piccadilly Institute, and Equinox. It was such a thriving business but sadly it was cut short due to the changes in London's licencing laws.

I think what works about our relationship is that, like me, she has big aspirations, and she works very hard. We also had the time to connect because we were working so closely with each other. Whenever I get an idea for a new business or idea, she'll firstly tell me I'm mad but then she'll be right there beside me helping me do it.

I now have three wonderful, beautiful children with her; Oliver, India and Spencer. My friend Oliver, the brains behind the modern-day Robin Hood scheme, was certainly a big inspiration when it came to naming my firstborn.

As he was our first child, and having a background in children's parties, I knew I had to do something special for Oliver's first birthday party, one to match the parties of the elite London folk I had spent years arranging. We went completely overboard and spent around £25,000 on the most lavish exciting kids party you could imagine. The story was even picked up by The Sun newspaper. It was held in an amazing venue in Bloomsbury owned by a close friend called Denis. He was always willing to do me a favour and he hired it to me for a discounted price. He owns an amazing events company called Awesome Events so it was great to have him involved. He is now India's godfather. The party was in a big top tent that could no doubt hold two football pitches inside it.

We divided the room in two, separating the most exciting attractions behind a curtain that we would later reveal. The kids walked in seeing a few decorations and a soft play area thinking that this was all they were to get; I loved seeing the eyes of the kids light up when we pulled back the curtain.

I also hired ten of our entertainers to walk around dressed as different characters; I wanted it to feel like Disneyland. We had a cinema wall playing kids cartoons, a bouncy castle, inflatables, a candy floss machine, a chocolate fountain and much more. My favourite memory was when I, dressed up as Woody from Toy Story, lifted Oliver onto my shoulders as our family and friends cut the birthday cake for him and everybody sang Happy Birthday. He was clapping along and was so happy to be the centre of attention. Over 250 guests attended that day, and everyone had a wonderful time.

As they grow older, I can see all of my children going into the performing arts as both Laura and I have. They all have London based agents and are already landing jobs. I feel like I will be handing over the baton and preparing them to be a success in whatever they choose to do. If they do decide to go into music or television, I'll hopefully be able to give them lots of advice and guidance and steer them away from some of the mistakes I've made over my career.

Not only have I been lucky in love and finally managed to settle down, but I've also been lucky with my friends. My old friend Garrick moved to the US a few years ago. I was so happy to see him get married in The Hamptons. I was one of his best men and Jon was the other (another apple thrower) . Laura and Oliver came with me to the wedding but they both went to bed quite early as Oliver was only tiny back then. Meanwhile, I stayed on downstairs enjoying the free bar. This is never a good idea, even at a wedding. I ended up getting drunk and passed out. Rather than leave me to stagger back to my room, as would normally happen in Britain, the Americans insisted on calling 911. The paramedics arrived and cut me out of the expensive tuxedo that I'd borrowed and took me to the hospital. The next morning, I wake up in hospital completely confused as to what has happened.

"You're fine," the nurses said, "we just wanted to monitor you. You can discharge yourself now." My first thought was to Laura and what she was going to think about me having drunk so much I needed to go to hospital. My next thought was about my attire. The tuxedo had disappeared, and I was in nothing but a hospital gown.

"Where are my clothes?" I demanded, by now more frustrated than disorientated.

"Sorry sir," they began, and they explained that since they'd cut me out of the tuxedo, they'd just chucked them away. It was a hired tuxedo, so I'd have to now pay for it.

I took a taxi back to the posh hotel in The Hamptons in

my gown hoping no one would see me as I sneaked up to my room. When I got there the place was empty. I didn't have pockets, let alone a room key. No one was answering as I was hammering on the door.

I panicked that Laura had got wind of my antics and been so annoyed with me that she'd just upped and left. There was little else I could do but traipse back down to reception, in my gown, to try and found out what had happened. They had simply moved Laura to a different room with Oliver so that they could avoid all the drama.

Of course, over breakfast, all the wedding guests wanted to know what had happened and it was very embarrassing. It was a good send-off for Garrick into married life and I was over the moon for him. The wedding and our enduring friendship showed us just how far we'd come from our school days in England. We now have a business together called Simply Baby Love LLC that sells child safety locks through Amazon in the US.

Today, things are a little slower than they once were because I'm focused on my young family. I continue to work as hard as I ever have but I enjoy spending as much time as I can with my children. It is important to have that balance.

I've been extremely fortunate to have the love and support of my mum, dad and sister throughout my journey. My sister, Charlotte, is a successful Hollywood actress and starred in a few blockbusters. A few years ago, she won the best-supporting actress in the National Film Awards in 2018 for her role as Karen in Scott and Sid. I was amazed and broke down in tears when I heard the news. For a while she lived in L.A, but she's recently moved back to London meaning she is closer to me. She has a lovely little boy of her own now, Thomas, my nephew who gets along very well with my three children. Meanwhile, Mum and Dad are both now happily retired and still living in the house I spent my teenage years growing up in. They've been the greatest support to me, no situation I find myself in, however outrageous or dangerous seems to phase them; they taught me the value of staying calm under pressure.

I have also been lucky enough to call some amazing people my friends. They have been with me through thick and thin. Some are named in the book already and others have not necessarily been named in this volume, but you know who you are and that you have all had a profound impact on my life. I remain ever grateful for that. I'm sure our stories and adventures together will be shared in subsequent volumes. I will always be there at the end of the phone or in-person if any of you ever need me and I am sure you all know that.

As this book is about to be published, I am embarking on many new and exciting business ventures. These include the global launch of a Parental First Aid Teddy Bear with Nick, and a brand new platform, developed with Stuart and

Neg, that offers virtual nights in with celebrities around the world. None of this would run as smoothly however, without my good friend and Business Manager, Natasha, who helps me implement and launch each crazy new idea I have, whilst also helping to oversee my other businesses on a daily basis.

I am also very proud of my new appointment into Global Protection Gateway, I have just joined forces and become a full Partner with my good friends Carl and Tony to combat the current Global PPE Crisis and together we have just formally signed a joint venture agreement with the Legendary 'Hilton' Family and America's First Response. Volume II should be an exciting read... Throughout the highs and the lows, there is one idea that's always stood me in good stead; you must get back up again when you get knocked down, and try even harder to succeed despite any hurdles in your way. It does not matter what the challenge is, if you work hard enough, and you believe in yourself then you will succeed.

I truly believe ANYTHING IS POSSIBLE...

Under One Roof London - Proudly created and founded by myself, Anne-Marie Martin and Laura James

Proud opening of Under One Roof Thanet with my partners Zahra & Parisa Tarjomani

Myself and Oliver on our New York Robin Hood Cash blowout trip. 'Modern Day Robin Hood'

Mum and I at my Sister's Wedding

Proud brother at my little sister's wedding

Jamie admiring my teeth...

Dad and I at my sister's wedding

My little Boy Spencer's first trip to London

Enjoying the red carpet

My beautiful Daughter India

Dad and I at an awards ceremony after my 'Greatest Showman' performance

Winning Best Street Dancer 2019 at National Championships - the old dog still has some moves…

My amazing Sister winning Best Supporting Actress in the National Film Awards for her role in 'Scott and Sid'

My Sassy little India

Oliver - just after signing with his first London agent. His book will be next

My World - Oliver, India and Spencer

Look out for volume II!

These are the companies I currently own and/or I am a partner in

StoryTerrace

www.ingramcontent.com/pod-product-compliance
Ingram Content Group UK Ltd.
Pitfield, Milton Keynes, MK11 3LW, UK
UKHW062313290726
14090UKWH00018B/1034